THE
LIVING
KITCHEN

THE
LIVING
KITCHEN

Organic Vegetarian Cooking
for Family and Friends

Jutka Harstein

Floris Books

Translated by Jutka Harstein, Adam Cohn and Jessica Wilson Genauer
First published in Hebrew under the title *Bishul Male Chaim (Cooking Full of Life)*
by Jutka Harstein, Harduf
This English edition published in 2012 by Floris Books
© 2009 Judith Harstein Cohn
This translation © Floris Books 2012

British Library CIP Data available
ISBN 978-086315-924-4
Printed in Poland

Thank you

To my grandmother Omama and to my mother who were my first cooking teachers.

To Ayelet Arnon for most of the illustrations and for endless hours of conversation about the book and about life.

To Adam, my son, who drew lots of fruits, vegetables and herbs after we realised, two weeks before the Hebrew book had to go to print, that there weren't enough drawings. Emergency was declared: Ayelet moved into our house, Adam put everything aside, days became nights and nights were spent in concentrated artistic activity. It was a special time watching these two artists sit next to each other and work in harmony so the 'birth' could happen. All I had to do was serve them good nourishing food, some less nourishing cakes and cookies, and lots of coffee and hot chocolate.

Adam and Ayelet also designed the artistic look of the pages in the original Hebrew edition.

To Noah Bareket, the editor of the Hebrew book, who accompanied me in the phases of 'pregnancy' with patience, and was my guide in creating order from the mountains of pages that had gathered on my desk during nine years of writing (the whole book was written by hand). She brought me down from the heights of creative euphoria to practical realities so the book could take physical shape.

To Dafna Cohen, the editor of the recipes, for the many hours spent composing and checking the recipes together with me.

To Ayelet Segal, the graphic designer, who accompanied me in the last phase of the 'birth', the hardest one, when the 'baby' starts to show itself in the physical world.

To Mrs Eleanor Arzieli (may she rest in peace), who was my English and creative writing teacher and encouraged me to write stories. Her counsel that 'good writing starts with clear thinking' accompanied me during the process of creating this book and helped me to gather the scattered pictures of my life into an organised frame.

To Limor, Amina, Ziv, Itai – the restaurant's team at different times – who all left recipes behind.

To Fatma Kaabia, who has been working with me for sixteen years in the restaurant, for her loyal support.

To Keren Berkowitz, who joined the team and became a partner.

To all my customers who waited patiently for this book and pushed me to bring it to light – to make it a reality.

To Helen, my house partner and best friend for five years in Forest Row, England. Together we created a life that nourished our sons and the many guests of our home with delicious meals, some of which can be found in this book.

To Johanna Baker, Ileana Botero and all the Nutley Hall residents for teaching me how to cook and eating my experiments.

To Dorothea, the biodynamic gardener at Michael Hall in Forest Row, who taught me to observe plants and to recognise the magic of life forces in them.

To my amazing cook friends – Caz (may she rest in peace), Vera, Laura, Helen, Moya – with whom I studied the deep meaning of food for five years.

To all my friends who accompanied me during the nine years of writing, listened to my stories, tried the recipes and advised me.

To Erez Serlin, 'my' farmer from Harduf, who is devoted to his ideals and grows vegetables full of life forces in the 'house garden'.

To my man, Fahed Najami, for giving me the love I have waited for all my life.

And last but not least, those that were also the first: the angels of the book who accompanied me and always helped me when I requested their assistance.

Thank yous for the English-language edition

To Auriol and Melinda de Smidt for their pure presence in my life and for editing my stories that were written in English but needed a native speaker's touch. They also polished all the other texts in the English edition.

To Jessica Wilson Genauer for translating part of the text from Hebrew to English.

Once again to Adam, my son, who translated many of the recipes.

To Katy Lockwood-Holmes and Sally Polson at Floris Books, who recognised what the book is and what it could be and who, along with Eleanor Collins, edited the English-language edition.

To Helena Waldron, who laid out this edition, and Chani McBain, who brought it to market, and to the whole team at Floris Books.

To work precisely, beautifully,
As the star passes through the sky;
So is worthy.

Dolgozni csak pontosan, szépen,
Ahogy a csillag megy az égen,
Úgy érdemes.

JÓZSEF ATTILA

Contents

Millilitres (ml)	U.S. fluid ounces (fl oz)
30	1
50	1.7
100	3.3
300	10.1
500	16.9
750	25.4
1000	33.8

We'd welcome your feedback…

All kitchens are different; ingredients vary in different parts of the world; some ovens cook slow, some fast. If you would like to tell us how one of these recipes worked for you and how we might improve it in future editions, we'd welcome your experience and feedback at floris@florisbooks.co.uk .

A note from the publisher of the English-language edition

This book has metric measurements (grams and millilitres) for European and Commonwealth readers, and U.S. cup equivalents for American readers. The U.S. cup measure is very close but not exactly the same as the imperial cup measure; however here the difference is of no significance, as the style of cooking does not call for minute precision.

Jutka herself prefers the convenience of cooking with cupfuls and spoonfuls – the cook scoops the ingredient directly from storage vessel to pot or bowl – and such measures allow for approximations and so for the cook's own taste and judgement.

In line with this style of cooking, a tablespoon (tbs) is an approximate rather than an exact measure in this book. Formal tablespoon measures vary in size by country and cooking tradition. Here we suggest you use a medium–large size spoon from your cutlery drawer.

These recipes have a home-kitchen informality that leaves plenty of room for experimenting and using your own experience to subtly adjust quantities and proportions.

We include centigrade and Fahrenheit oven temperatures throughout, as well as metric and imperial lengths for cake tins and baking dishes.

Vegan recipes

Recipes free from dairy products and eggs are marked with a 'V' for vegan next to their title. Some *do* contain honey, so that our vegan readers can make their own choices about this ingredient.

Introduction

God's greatest gift to me is a life filled with colour and transformations.

I grew up on Hungarian food. This consisted mostly of different parts of the pig, which would be slaughtered in the courtyard of our home on a freezing winter day. I have undergone a long journey from being the young girl, gripped with emotion, staring at the sharp knife as it searched for the right point to kill the squealing pig, to being the woman welcoming her customers to her vegetarian restaurant serving organic food full of life. Yet my memories from my childhood are all positive. It is true I had to stand in a long queue every morning in communist Romania for milk and bread. But, on the other hand, everything was home-made because the shops were empty. So food – especially because it was made by Omama (Granny) – was delicious.

My relationship to simple food that is grown and cooked with love, my belief in living and cooking without waste, the feeling of harmony and gratefulness for everything that I have, are only a small part of the inheritance of my childhood. The rest you will find in my stories and you will eat through the recipes in this book.

Cooking was never a career for me. In fact I am not built for definitions, so all the things I have done have happened as an organic part of life. It is hard to put a finger on when I became a cook, but I first prepared meals for people outside my family while living in a kibbutz (a community in Israel) in 1979. I was in charge of the vegetarian lunches for 150 people. To help me overcome my total ignorance of such cooking, my American mother-in-law, Ateret Cohn, sent me *The Moosewood Cookbook*, then a new bestseller.

That book altered the way I thought about food. I became so ardent about vegetarianism that my then husband had to say, 'Food is not everything.' But for me it was. Later, when, after divorce, I had to support my only son, Adam, I cooked for people privately to add to my wages as an English teacher. In 1990 I went to Forest Row in East Sussex, England, to study anthroposophical education. I got a job as a cook at Nutley Hall, a home for people with special needs. There I could practise what I was learning in my weekly study-group with all the cooks of the area. My colleagues opened a new dimension of food for me by carefully observing vegetables, recognising the life forces and the formative forces in them, and understanding that FOOD IS SPIRIT. If *The Moosewood Cookbook* was my high school, those years in Forest Row and Nutley Hall were my university! The best that exists! The doctorate was Harduf's Restaurant (later I will tell you how I ended up there); this book is my thesis. And you will award the mark!

It is not possible to create new recipes. All recipes are ancient ones that are created anew and changed a little. Sometimes they are received straight from God (if he finds you worthy). Cookbooks are only inspiration and suggestion. You are invited to take the recipes offered in my book, change them, add to them and make them your own.

Through food we unite. If you cook according to the recipes in this book I will be present in your kitchen. I experience this as a great honour. This is the reason why every person who would like a recipe from my restaurant receives it. That is exactly how this book began. At first I copied out every recipe by hand for every customer who requested one. When the requests increased I photocopied pages of recipes to distribute them. At the same time I began to write stories about my childhood and about my mother. They simply came to me and asked to be included in my cooking book.

This book is written out of love for healthy food, according to my world-view. I am very influenced by anthroposophy and it is an important tool in my personal spiritual development, but this is not an anthroposophical cookbook, for better or for worse. Whether you love and adopt the recipes in this book or whether you do not, there is no connection to anthroposophical written knowledge, only to my personal interpretation of it.

Different people need different types of food. There are those who need raw food, others macrobiotic food, meat or vegetarian. Taste and smell are very personal and I honour the place of every one of you and know that it is always possible to continue developing.

I have been writing this book for nine years. Just as the baby must emerge from the mother's womb, this book must be finished. There is no choice. The contractions are so strong that sometimes I wake up at four in the morning to write. I know that very soon the book will appear on paper. How will it be, I will only know when I hold it in my hands. However, unlike a first baby that we do not want to give to anyone else, this one I happily share with you, hoping that you enjoy it as much as I enjoyed writing it.

Hallelujah.

Jutka Harstein
Harduf, 2008

An addition to the English-language edition

Writing a book is a very exciting process. However, even more important is the meeting between the book and the people who read it. A cookbook has yet another dimension because I believe if you do not cook from my book at all we have missed each other, and that is sad. My absolute aim with the book was to touch you on such a deep level, through putting many pictures of my life in front of you, that you will want to 'eat' me! And that means you want to cook from this book and eat the food. Sharing your cooking with other people will make me even happier! If on your festive dinner table there are a few dishes from my living kitchen, then I feel that I am sharing that moment with all of you!

In Israel a surprising number of people have embraced the book. It is still selling as it was three years ago. This gave me the idea of publishing it in English, so it can reach even more people.

Food awareness is growing, but also becoming very hysterical. I often feel sorry for people who put themselves on almost impossible diets, not for the sake of losing weight but out of fear of certain foods. Hopefully this book will provide you with the right tools to remember who you are – to connect you to your pure, essential self, who bravely chooses to nourish body, soul and spirit.

Hallelujah.

Jutka Harstein
Harduf 2012

The source of nourishment

On a lazy Sunday morning I entered my storeroom to sort out some boxes that were patiently waiting for me. They contained old porcelain cups and other kitchen utensils that I had inherited from my dearest aunt, Teri, who had passed away two years before. As I was going through these items from another world, I remembered what an awful cook she was. There were stories in the family about her burnt chicken, overcooked vegetables, cakes that never rose and brown goulash that was supposed to be red. Indeed she hated being in the kitchen so much that she only prepared meals when she had to, and with great resistance.

On the other hand she was one of the most interesting, intelligent, positive and warm-hearted people I have ever met. I was so utterly nourished by her inspiring personality that only when I left her house in the evening after a visit did I realise we had spent the whole day together without eating anything. We would discuss everything connected to life, starting from love, family problems and philosophy, and ending with art and education. But we never talked about food.

My source of inspiration for cooking came from my grandmother, Omama. She was the opposite of my aunt in all ways: not only was it impossible to converse with her about any intellectual matter, her whole life was centred on cooking. She entered the kitchen in the early morning and emerged from it in the late afternoon, when she sank into her deck chair in the garden and did crosswords until the evening.

She never liked us kids hanging around her kitchen too much; our 'dirty hands' were not allowed to help because we would 'ruin it all'. She had no patience for any nonsense in the kitchen. If she was in a good mood she allowed me to sit and watch her wash the vegetables and herbs for the soup, prepare the dough for fresh pasta, pluck the feathers of the chicken that was slaughtered by the neighbour in the early morning, mix sauces, bake cakes and biscuits, and make pancakes with vanilla cream in them. She was definitely the best cook on earth.

From the point of view of my nutritional knowledge today, the food I grew up on was not at all healthy. Yet I was absolutely nourished by it. And this was not because I had a special soul and spirit relationship with Omama, for I did not. In fact it took me many years to overcome my anger towards her, because she was stone hearted. It took lots of tearful moments for me to understand that there are people whose heart is made so hard by life that they cannot take their grandchildren onto their lap and hug them, but they might cook the best meals for them day after day without ever complaining about it.

I would like to dedicate this book to my Aunt Teri and to my grandmother, Omama, through whom I learnt that the source of nourishment is endless.

A Taste of Home

Mother's roses

I am at home. Mother is pottering around in the garden, weeding the spring vegetables she planted a few weeks ago. Her chickens are peacefully strolling around her. In a few hours, at twilight, she will cry out 'pee-pee-pee pee-pee', making a special sound they know well and will pass on to the next generation. The little ones are born with a built-in recognition that this sound is calling them for supper. Then invariably comes quarrelling time. Mother insists on putting the chicks to bed herself: it is not a task she will hand over. She tries to get them into their wobbly cage but they always make trouble, either because they are not sleepy or just to satisfy her need for a good quarrel.

She has lived alone for the twenty years since all her children left home, in an old country house that my great-grandfather built in the middle of our estate. There are no other houses around and, except for Janos, who bought half of the house, Mother goes days without having anyone to talk to. So she converses with her chickens and Sherry, her dog.

She wakes up every morning at six o'clock knowing there is so much to do that a day is never enough. Her garden is very large. A big plot has vegetables in it: onions, garlic, dill, parsley, tomatoes, peppers, aubergines (eggplants), peas and beans. There are lots of fruit trees, starting with

cherries, plums, pears and apricots, and ending with gooseberry and raspberry bushes. But the larger part of the garden is full of shrubs and flower beds, especially roses.

This is the first time for 25 years that I am at home in the spring. Before this visit I had told Mother on the phone that I might skip my regular summer visit this year and come in the winter instead. There was a moment of silence in which my heart started to sink with hers and then in a trembling voice she said, 'But Jutka, then you won't see my roses in full bloom.' In front of my eyes the well-planned Greek island summer holiday faded, and was replaced with yellow, orange, red, pink and white roses filling my nostrils with the best scent in the world: mother's roses. I knew I would be back in the summer.

I am sitting in a deck chair in the garden. Mother passes by wearing Bermuda shorts with big red and blue flowers on them, and a bra. When she was about 55 years old she got menopausal heat flushes, took her shirt off, and has refused to put one on ever since, except when she goes out to town. 'It is like a bikini,' she argues with us, as if it was totally normal for a 76-year-old woman weighing 90 kilos to wear a bikini. When my older sister became good friends with the mayor of our town, and he started visiting our summer house with his wife, we begged Mother to put a shirt on, but she calmly replied, 'He will have to get used to it.' Which he did. In fact eating my mother's food and relaxing in her garden became the rare happy moments of his life.

I am still sitting in the deck chair. Mother by now is in the kitchen rolling pasta, which we will eat with ground-up nuts and sugar. I close my eyes and do not want this moment ever to pass. I am holding my breath back as the most horrifying certainty grasps my heart: one day I will be sitting here, twilight will descend, but the chickens will not come running to eat their supper. Mother will not be there to call them. To stop my tears I run into the kitchen, put my arms around her and give her a big kiss. She smiles.

Mother died one month after this summer visit in which I smelt her roses.

Separation and meeting

When Mother died I took the first plane from Israel, rushing to the summer house I had left only a few weeks earlier. I could not believe my eyes. I had left in the middle of August when summer was at its peak. Mother and I had eaten as many of the ripe pears, peaches and plums as we could. Now, on the first day of October, a fading sun was waiting for me, the trees were losing their yellowed leaves, the air carried the smell of decaying nature and Mother was not there. All her flowers had withered in the garden. I could hardly find a small bunch to take to her funeral and lay on her chest inside the coffin, so that she would be buried with part of the earth she loved so much.

After the funeral my brother, my three sisters and I roamed the garden searching for something that we will never find again. Nobody's children, orphaned forever.

When I was left alone in the house I climbed into Mother's gigantic wardrobe and inhaled the smell of her clothes, uniting with her through the leftovers of her life body. Then I buried my face into the pillow she had lain on only a day earlier, trying to find the remnants of her warmth. Suddenly I understood that the light that gave me life had gone and from now on I would need to find the fire from within to cook the ingredients of my life into an edible stew. I was interrupted by the call of Mother's hungry chickens. I straightened myself, dried my face, and went to feed them with corn.

Hungarian meal

Our nutritional habits reflect our deepest identity. Although I was born a Hungarian from Transylvania, which is part of Romania, I no longer define myself as belonging to that nation. In fact I do not belong to any nation or religion. I spent many years trying to decide whether I am Christian like my mother or Jewish like my father. Finally, after being unable to disconnect from one in order to belong to the other, I decided that it is best to be free from both. As concerns nationality, whether I am Hungarian or Israeli, naturally I am both and neither. I love *rakott krumpli* and hummus. But neither is part of my everyday eating habits. The only thing that matters to me about what I put in my mouth is that it is 'good food'. Which basically means nourishing food with life forces.

In this book you can follow my nutritional journey. It was a long one, sometimes strict about no dairy, no eggs, no this or that, until I reached the present state in which I eat whatever I feel like. In my usual daily life in Israel I would not choose a single one of the dishes from the Hungarian meal. They belong to my past. Still, several times a year I happily return to my past and enjoy the dishes of my childhood. So, a few hours after I land in Budapest, I simply have to taste the heavenly flavour of the Esterházy torte from my favourite bakery-café, Ruszwurm, which has been serving cakes since 1827. Afterwards I go to visit with family, where I know that my sister has prepared *rakott krumpli* in my honour.

Hungarian Meal

HUNGARIAN GREEN BEAN SOUP
(Zöld paszuly leves)

HUNGARIAN SALAD (v)
(Ili saláta)

HUNGARIAN CUCUMBER SALAD (v)
(Uborka saláta)

RAKOTT KRUMPLI

ESTERHÁZY TORTE
(Eszterházy torta)

Hungarian green bean soup (Zöld paszuly leves)

Anyu, my mother, taught me how to make this soup. The lovage we put in this soup here in Israel I used to bring from Romania in a quantity that would last me for the entire year. My mother grew it in her garden and dried it for me. After her death I was worried: how will I make the soup without it? Fortunately, I found the herb in a nursery close to my house in Israel.

Serves 8

250 g (9 oz) green beans (yellow are also possible), pinch off the ends and break into desired length
1 red pepper (bell pepper), finely sliced
2 stalks (ribs) of celery with leaves, chopped
4 large tomatoes, chopped
3 stalks (ribs) of lovage (if you can't find lovage, use celery)
water or stock

Put all the vegetables in an iron pot, add water or stock until the vegetables are just covered, then add another 480 ml (2 cups) water or stock. Simmer, covered, until the beans are soft.

olive oil or butter for frying
2 medium onions, finely sliced
half a bulb of garlic, peeled and finely chopped
1 tbs flour (we used white but now I use wholewheat)
1 tbs sweet paprika

Fry the onion in the fat until golden. Add the garlic, flour and paprika. Stir. Slowly add some of the soup's liquid and cook, whisking for a few minutes, until you get a smooth liquid paste.

Add the paste to the soup and bring to the boil. Lower the heat.

1 tsp salt, or to taste

2 tbs brown sugar

2 tbs apple cider vinegar or lemon juice

3 tbs tomato paste

240 ml (1 cup) cream or sour cream

1 bunch of chopped dill or parsley or both

While stirring add the salt, sugar, vinegar or lemon juice and the tomato paste. At the end, pour in the cream, making sure the soup is no longer boiling.

Turn off the heat and add the herbs.

Lovage is a herb that looks a bit like celery but differs in taste. The Hungarians from Transylvania (which belongs to Romania) know this herb as *leostyan* because the Romanians use it in their national soup called *ciorba*. Some good things can result from living together!

Hungarian salad (Ili saláta) (V)

I learnt this salad from Ili, my sister-in-law.

Make this one day ahead of time.

Serves 6–8

half a red cabbage, finely shredded
1 large carrot, roughly shredded
half a celeriac, peeled and roughly shredded

Put into a bowl.

The marinade

1 tbs honey
3 tbs olive oil
salt and black pepper
juice of a lemon
pinch of grated nutmeg

Combine and pour onto the vegetables.
Chill.

Hungarian cucumber salad (Uborka saláta) (v)

Serves 4–6

6 large cucumbers, very finely cut
½ tbs salt
2 tbs sugar
60 ml (¼ cup) boiling water
60 ml (¼ cup) good-quality apple vinegar
a quarter of a bunch of dill, chopped
4–5 spring onions (scallions), sliced OR 1 red onion, finely sliced
sweet or hot paprika

1. Mix the cucumbers with the salt. Let them stand
    for 5 minutes.
2. Melt the sugar in the boiling water and cool.
3. Add the melted sugar, vinegar, dill and spring onions
    to the cucumbers.
4. Before serving, sprinkle some sweet or hot paprika
    on the salad.

Rakott krumpli

Rakott krumpli is a classic Hungarian potato casserole. We Transylvanians add cauliflower to it and I replace the sausage Hungarians use with sweet potatoes. The dish is really delicious even without the sweet potato.

Serves 6–8
Because this casserole is layered, you need a deep 23 x 35 cm (9 x 14 in) baking dish.

¾ kg (1 ½ lb) white potatoes, washed but not peeled
1 large sweet potato, whole
5 eggs, whole
500 g (1 lb) cauliflower, broken into florets

Take a deep cooking pot. Place the unpeeled potatoes at the bottom. Put the sweet potato, the cauliflower florets and the eggs on the potatoes. Cover with water so the eggs on the top are also covered. Bring to the boil and cook for 20 minutes.

Take out the eggs, cauliflower florets and sweet potatoes. With a knife, check if the potatoes are ready. If the knife goes through them easily, they are ready. If they are not ready, cook them for another 5–10 minutes. Cool all the ingredients. Don't overcook them! But if you do, just go on without panicking.

500 ml (16 US fl oz) sour cream (you could use yogurt or single (light) cream)
60 ml (1/4 cup) sunflower oil
1 tsp salt

Mix.

Putting the casserole together

Preheat your oven to 180° C (350° F).

Oil the baking dish with a brush.

If your potatoes are organic there is no need to peel them. Cut them into finger-thick slices. Place half of the potato slices in the baking dish. Slice all the cauliflower florets and the peeled hard-boiled eggs and layer them over the potatoes. Slice the sweet potato to make the next layer, and place the remaining half quantity of potato slices on top. Pour on the sour-cream mixture. If your sour cream is very thick, you can add a bit of milk to thin it.

Bake for 1 hour until the top is brown.

Can be served with steamed red cabbage (see page 164) and a rich vegetable salad.

Kids love this dish!

Once I made *rakott krumpli* but I didn't have cauliflower so I replaced it with broccoli. The result was delumptious!

Esterházy torte (Eszterházy torta)

A delicious but quite complex Hungarian delicacy, definitely the one I always choose in my favourite café in Budapest: Ruszwurm.

Your first problem is you need four round, 28 cm (11 in) diameter cake tins. If you don't have enough, borrow from your neighbours. If you can't, you can bake them one after the other.

Make this torte one day ahead. It needs 24 hours in the refrigerator to set.

Preheat the oven to 230° C (450° F).

The base

6 egg whites (save the yolks!)
200 g (1 cup) brown sugar
⎱ Beat until stiff.

100 g (1 ¼ cups) finely ground walnuts
2 tbs wholemeal flour
⎱ Mix and fold into the egg whites, keeping as much air in the mix as possible.

Oil the 4 cake tins and pour into them equal amounts of the nut-and-egg white mixture. Bake for 7 minutes.

With the help of a knife remove the baked torte layers from the tins immediately after taking them out of the oven.

Vanilla cream with nuts

600 ml (2 ½ cups) milk

150 g (¾ cup) brown sugar

5 tbs flour

6 egg yolks (the ones you saved from the egg whites above!)

3 tbs water

200 g (7 oz) butter, softened

85 g (1 cup) finely ground hazelnuts

2 tbs real rum

1 tbs vanilla essence (extract)

1. Boil the milk and sugar.
2. In a bowl, combine the flour, egg yolks and water. Mix them with a whisk until they are smooth. Slowly pour them into the hot milk and whisk non-stop for a few minutes. Cook this mixture on a low heat while whisking until it bubbles. Turn off the heat and cool completely. Whisk from time to time to avoid skin forming on the top.
3. Whip the butter in a separate bowl. Add to it the cooled milky mixture, the nuts, rum and vanilla. Mix well.

Constructing the torte

1. Place one baked and cooled torte layer on your serving plate or tray. Spread a bit less than a quarter of the cream on it. Place on this another layer and spread another almost quarter of the cream. Repeat this process twice more.
2. Use the leftover cream for spreading on the sides of the torte. Sprinkle ground nuts on the top.
3. Chill the torte in the refrigerator for 24 hours before serving.
4. Serve with whipped cream.

Foundations and Understandings

Humans are upside-down plants

The nutrition of human beings is directly connected to the plant kingdom. Plants don't only provide us with oxygen; in them is hidden the source of all our food. Animals are also dependent on plants. Thus when we consume animal products we are indirectly nourished by the food they ate. Without plants, life could not exist on earth.

In order to understand what nutrition (nourishment) is and how it affects the human being, it is necessary to look at the development of the plant from its beginning as a small seed in the earth until its culmination as a ripe fruit that contains the seeds of the next plant.

The plant is built up by nature's forces: sun, earth, water and air. The plant's roots suck up (feed on) minerals straight from the earth and the stem passes these minerals to the highest parts of the plant. The leaves receive the sun's rays (light) and with their help transforms the carbon (C), that is in the plant as CO_2, into material that builds the physical body of the plant. Plants are the only 'creatures' on earth that can build their body in this way – directly from the minerals of the earth, turning sunlight to substance.

A good cook should follow the development of the growing plant, since cooking starts in the garden, the sun being a master chef. The German poet Frederich Schiller said, 'Do you seek the highest, the greatest?

The plant can teach you.'* There is a lot to be learned watching the process in which one part of the plant turns into a different part, thus creating a never-ending metamorphosis. Cooking is a high form of alchemy and so is the developing plant. In both, one thing becomes another. We put inedible grains and water into a pot, heat them with the fire of our stove, and they become edible.

In the plant world we can observe the metamorphoses each part of the plant goes through. As soon as the seed sprouts, it disappears and becomes root and stem. The long, round stem broadens into a leaf that has a flat form. On the top the plant is crowned by the colourful queen, the flower, which developed from the leaves. Here, in stamen and pistil, the plant turns more inward and in a process of contraction and hardening it prepares the goal of its development in fruit and seed formation. The seed is not only the end of the development of the flower but also the beginning of the next plant.

When the seed gets the right elements – moisture and warmth – it transforms into a sprout that, as small as it is, can push the hard earth aside to make space for the root that it becomes. When we think about this, we can see what strength is in seeds and roots and why it is so healthy to eat them.

Roots grow downward, towards the centre of the earth, under the forces of gravity. The dark, cool, moist earth determines their firm texture, grey or white colour and contracting qualities. The stem and the first leaves, the cotelydons, burst forth seeking the sun, revealing themselves to our eyes in their greenness, which they get through photosynthesis from their interaction with the sun. Hard material is dissolved, form is expanded as the plant is freed from the jail of the earth and meets air and straight rays of sun. Colourfulness, the most visual expression of the heavenly forces, belongs to the upper part of the plant, the flower and fruit. Exceptional roots such as the carrot, the beetroot (beet) and the radish bring us not only earthiness in their flavours but also a flower quality in their colours, which are more closely connected to light and warmth. For this reason it is highly recommended to use them in our daily food.

* Frederich Schiller, *Das Höchste (The Supreme)*

Leaves are connected to air and light: through them we eat the 'airiness' of the world. Some leaves have a light airy quality, like spinach, dill, parsley and curly lettuce. In other leaves, like Swiss chard, the airiness is mixed with earth forces. White and red cabbage has the harshest earthy quality among leaves, so it is the hardest to digest, causing unpleasant gas formation. When assembling a nourishing meal it is important to take this into account. A heavy meal, for example, should be well balanced with a salad of airy leaves. In the same way, a meal with a light main dish will be happily balanced with an 'earthy' cabbage and carrot salad.

The leaves are the lungs of the plant: in photosynthesis, they receive sunlight and transform it into material. They absorb carbon dioxide from the air. The plant uses the carbon to create its body, and releases oxygen, which human beings need for breathing. In every place in the world that lacks 'the lungs' of plants, the quality of the air and oxygen decreases and there is a real threat to the existence of life. The leaf also acts as an agent maintaining the equilibrium of the plant, standing between two opposing forces: the root, which grows downward, and the flower and the fruit, which pull the plant upwards towards the sun.

The forces of the sun work most forcefully on the highest part of the plant: the flower, the fruit and the seeds that are contained within it. As the seed ripens in the sun, it turns from being soft to hard. When it is the ripest it is also the hardest, containing the most sun forces. In order for it to be suitable for human food it needs to be softened again by cooking, which is, in fact, a continuation of the sun's work.

The plant's forces of fertility are contained in the seed. Its development in the moist, dark earth can be compared to the development of a fetus in its mother's warm, dark womb. Like the seed that needs cooking to become edible, the baby also needs further 'cooking' (phases of development), until it can stand in the world, feet on the ground, its heart feeling secure, capable of loving, knowing who it is and what it wants from itself and from its environment.

The plant is a threefold form with its root, leaf and flower as described above. The human being also has a threefold body: head, rhythmical system (heart and lungs) and digestive and reproductive system (limbs).

A similarity and correspondence exists between the plantand humans. The most mineral part of the plant is its roots, which also have some hair (you might not know this since today it is really hard to find a carrot or beetroot (beet) that is not pre-washed, a process that inevitably takes away not only the hair but washes out some of the precious life forces). Similarly, the most mineral, hardened part of the human body is the head (with hair on it). The plant breathes through its leaves just as humans do through their lungs, which look like trees with trunk and branches. Continuing the resemblance, we can see the way in which the upper part of the plant is home for the formation of its 'baby', the fruit, with seed formation being its final aim. Our lower reproductive system with the seed in the womb produces a baby.

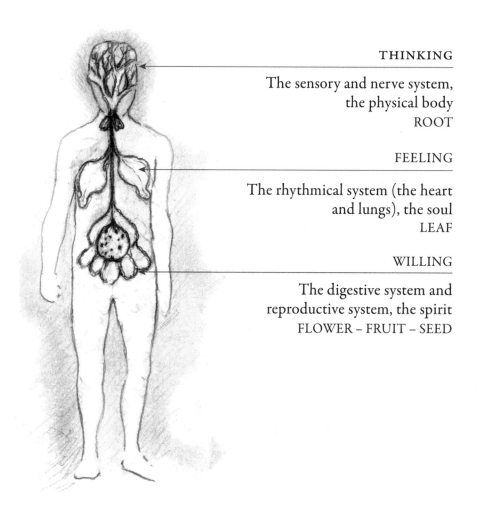

THINKING

The sensory and nerve system,
the physical body
ROOT

FEELING

The rhythmical system (the heart
and lungs), the soul
LEAF

WILLING

The digestive system and
reproductive system, the spirit
FLOWER – FRUIT – SEED

This picture of the connection between the human being and the plant brings to light that the human being is an upside-down plant. Our most mineral part, our head, turns upwards, towards the sky, while the hardest part of the plant, its root, is pulled towards the depth of the earth. Our internal reproductive organs are hidden while the plant's exposed reproductive organs (which provide us so much pleasure with the beauty of flowers and fruit) turn upwards. Our middle realm, heart and lung, is responsible for the interchange between the air without and within through our breathing and the rhythm of our blood, thus keeping our body in a healthy balance.

The ego, the essence of our being, lives on the stream of the blood and through our feeling connects thinking and willing. Similarly, the leaf – which corresponds to our middle realm – is the harmoniser of the plant.

What do we learn from this picture as cooks? It is that a healthy, balanced meal should contain all the parts of the plant, ensuring that we receive all the nourishment we need for our physical body (the head), soul (middle realm) and spirit (digestive and reproductive system).

The plant's roots nourish our head where deep thoughts dwell.

The plant's leaves nourish our rhythmic system and are important for the healthy functioning of the lungs and heart, the home of feelings.

The flower, the fruit and the seed nourish our digestive and reproductive systems. They supply us with vital energy for work and creativity, with the help of our will.

The world provides us with an abundance of edible representatives of all these parts of the plant.

Roots, represented by the carrot, are always a desirable addition to any salad or dish. Beetroot (beet), kohlrabi, radish, celeriac and parsley root will also contribute to any salad, soup or dish. So will parsnip, turnip and horseradish.

Leaves are easily recognised and used by most of us. We happily eat all kinds of lettuces (quite amazing how many kinds have been grown lately), baby and mustard leaves, rocket (arugula) leaves (keep away from the pre-washed ones and do not feel embarrassed to ask for fresh ones), celery, parsley, coriander (cilantro) and the ones you would not consider a leaf, but they are: onion and garlic.

Flowers are the difficult part of the meal. Broccoli and cauliflower can be added to a soup or dish. Drinking a flower tea such as hibiscus, rose, chamomile and others can be a good way to include flowers in the meal. The hibiscus drink that we serve in the restaurant is a great option to be integrated into every meal (the last recipe in the book).

Fruits exist in abundance. Almost all common and popular vegetables – such as tomato, cucumber, courgette (zucchini), aubergine (eggplant), pumpkin, butternut and pepper – are in fact fruits. And the classic fruits transform any meal into a colourful, sweet delight.

Grains, which comprise an essential and basic component for every meal are **seeds**. The section of this book entitled 'The seven grains' will guide you through the different aspects and qualities of grains.

The life of the plant between the polarities of darkness and light, contraction and expansion, coldness and warmth is also expressed in its taste, flavour, aroma and scent. Through them a sort of discussion develops between the heavenly, cosmic forces, the plant and human beings.

Aristotle defined seven tastes that appear in the plant kingdom: acidic (sour); bitter and harsh, which are found mostly in roots; salty (I mean as a taste, not the mineral), which is found mostly in leaves; sweet, spicy (sharp) and oily, which are found mostly in flowers, fruits and seeds.

Dandelion and chicory are bitter, celery and parsley root are harsh and acidy, contracting our mouths less than bitterness. The saltiness of leaves can be tasted in lettuce, celery, lemon balm tea, parsley and others, while the sweetness of fruits does not need explanation: you have all eaten mango, pear, grapes, apples and an endless list of others. Most seeds are oily – sunflower seeds, flaxseeds, corn, nuts, almonds and others – while sharpness (spiciness) is found in mustard seeds, peppercorns, cardamom seeds, cumin and a long list of others.

Of course many flavours that belong to one part of the plant can be found in other parts as well. Spices, herbs and vegetables rarely have one simple taste. Carrot and beetroot (beet) are sweet, radish and mustard leaves are spicy, some fruits and berries are sour, and some leaves – like lavender, rosemary and geranium – are oily (they are good for use in massage). We need great awareness and attention to differentiate the subtle nuances of tastes. The time has come for us to look for quality in real tastes rather than giving in to the abuse of our taste buds by the food industry. A good cook can season dishes well only after they have taught themselves the art of tasting the seven flavours separately.

In the menus in this book I endeavour to ensure that every meal contains each part of the plant. There are diverse tastes and colours, to ensure that every part of the human being will be nourished.

The plant and the human being live in coexistence and mutual dependency. Plants are the source of our nourishment and the provider of our necessary oxygen. We give them the carbon dioxide with which they build their body. We also affect them, through our relationship with nature. The health of plants depends on the health of the entire world. The more balanced the earth, air, water and warmth of the sun, the more nutritious plants will be for us. Our role in the ecological balance is well known. We have a moral responsibility towards plants – they provide us with life and it is up to us to care for their health.

Cooking and the digestive system

On the left side of the following diagram is the process of the building of the plant. As we saw in the previous section, the plant builds its body directly through a connection with the forces of nature (minerals, air, water, heat, the planets and more). After the 'foundation' of the plant has been built, it reaches its climax. From a biological point of view the peak is always the seeding; in our nutrition, it is when the part of the plant we want to eat is ripe.

When this point passes, the life forces of the plant flow to other parts, while the part we want to eat is weakened, its taste changes and it often becomes inedible. When the carrot plant goes to seed formation (which happens after its root is ripe), its life forces are found in the flower and not in the root that we want to eat. Similarly, when the lettuce plant goes to seed formation its leaves become bitter and inedible.

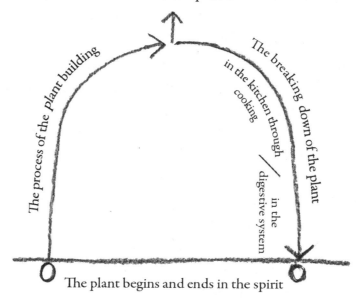

The climax: ripeness

The process of the plant building

The breaking down of the plant

in the kitchen through
cooking

in the
digestive system

The plant begins and ends in the spirit

We can easily identify when fruit is ripe – it changes its colour and its taste becomes sweet. Unfortunately most fruits that are sold today are picked long before that point and are artificially ripened. The need to transport fruit over long distances leads to an early harvest and unnatural ripening process, which wastes immense resources. This is one reason why we should buy fruit and vegetables at a nearby market from local growers.

If we left a fruit – an apple, for example – on the tree after it had ripened, eventually it would over-ripen, fall to the ground, decompose, disintegrate and turn into earth. Its apple-like quality would disappear.

But if we do not leave it on the tree, but pick it at its peak when its life forces are greatest, bring it to our kitchen, cook it and then eat it, the decomposing process will happen in our kitchen and then in our bodies.

Cooking is a continuation of the work of the sun. The more cooked the food is, the more it disintegrates and the easier it is to digest. Babies, elderly people and ill people, for example, need food that is more cooked, in order to help their weak digestive systems.

For healthy people, over-cooking can weaken and stagnate our digestive system. Raw food that is not cooked at all, like salad or fruit, makes us work hard to decompose it, thus giving us strength for dealing with life. Their consumption is highly recommended in our daily meals.

When we cook, the type of heat that we use is very important. It is important not to 'break' the life forces of the plant with unnatural heat. It is advisable to use heat that is similar in essence to the sun, which was the plant's first 'cook'. Sun ovens, campfires and wood stoves are the most ancient and best methods of cooking. The Aga in England was a blessing! In most homes gas has replaced the old methods and is an acceptable (ecologically quite clean) compromise. The electric hotplate and electric oven are less good (energy in them is far from the source), but still acceptable.

The modern microwave oven uses a completely different method. Microwaves work by moving the molecules of a substance very rapidly to create heat. This is a strange and unnatural intervention in the natural process of the plant. The microwaves interfere and change the composition of the food using a method that changes its nature completely. This confuses the plant causing it to lose its life forces, so that what remains on our plate is only dead material which lacks life, the very reason for our food consumption. Warming food up in a microwave gives similar results.

The cooking instruments are important as well. If the pots, pans and baking dishes and trays are made of natural materials, they allow a more natural and healthy cooking process. Iron cooking utensils are the best. Clay is also good, as well as glass and stainless steel. Teflon is a problematic material. If the Teflon non-stick coating becomes cracked, it can become toxic and dangerous. Aluminium (aluminum) is a toxic material that enters the cooking food and can poison us. Nowadays there are many good materials on the market. I personally love my iron pots and iron frying-pan and would not replace them for anything!

Let's return to the diagram.

After the plant has ripened in nature and been cooked in the kitchen, the process of decomposition is continued in our digestive system until the food disappears and becomes our flesh and our body.

When we approach food it is good to give the digestive system time to prepare itself. Firstly, the sense of smell is active. A pleasant smell of food causes the secretion of saliva and digestive juices. Sometimes smelling particular aromas creates desire for the food identified with them. The appearance of food is very important because we also eat with our eyes. If the plate does not look good, or if the food has a strange colour or appearance, we lose our appetite. The thought of desired food, the smell and look of it are essential elements in the digestion. Before the food reaches our mouth, the digestive system is ready and prepared for it.

Our teeth are the original food processors, grinding and pulverising; they need to do their job thoroughly, ensuring that we can get the most nourishment out of our meal and feel satisfied.

After smelling, seeing and chewing the food, we swallow it and it begins its journey in the digestive system, which is the deepest and most hidden system in our bodies. In the stomach and in the intestines, the food meets with the digestive juices and different enzymes that decompose it. In this process the life forces that have built the plant are freed.

This cannot happen if we do not have a force from within that makes the whole system work. The etheric or life forces of the human body come to meet the plant and transform it. Flora and fauna bacteria also help in the process. They are strengthened by certain foods (natural yogurt) and weakened by antibiotics, for example. Nourishing food that we consumed the day before contributes to the strengthening of our existing life forces.

There are people with weak digestion while others have no such problems. At all times it is extremely important to understand which food is giving you this inner strength to turn an orange-coloured carrot into your red blood. It is very important to maintain a strong and healthy digestive system! The more the digestive force is active, the stronger it becomes. Cooked food does not demand such hard work in our digestion as raw food. Processed food that is already broken down causes degeneration of the digestive system. Children who are fed on junk food have weaker digestive systems. Strengthening it means gradually moving to healthy food, which will awaken their digestive forces.

The process of decomposition ends at the intestinal wall. The broken-down food is on one side of the intestine – the apple or carrot that we ate – and can be identified as such. On the other side it disappears and turns into our blood. At this point the process of alchemy has reached its peak: one kind of material (carrot) has turned into a different one (our blood and eventually our flesh). The world that is outside of us became us.

Food, which started in the spiritual world, just as we began, became material in the form of a seed. It developed into edible foodstuff, the human being decomposed it in its digestive system, and at the end of the process completely 'stripped' it of its material form. The green lettuce cannot become our red blood unless it loses all its material substance at our intestinal wall, thus becoming spirit (nothing, zero point). One form of material can become a totally different form only if it goes through this transformation of letting go, to the point of nothing. The process of spirit – the beginning of all existence – becoming material (food), its transformation back into spirit (at the intestinal wall) and its formation again into physicality (our body) is one of the greatest wonders of life on earth.

From what are we nourished? From the material itself? From the body of the plant that we eat? Or from the spirit and life forces that exist within it? Physically, only a small part of the food remains inside us. What feeds us and becomes us are the spirit and life forces. Therefore the richer the life forces in the food that we eat, the more it will nourish us.

We become what we eat. But from a deeper point of view we eat who we are. Our choice of one food or another shows us where we are in our spiritual development, which is our deep relationship to ourselves and to the world. A person who cannot give up 'bad' food simply is not 'there' yet. Do not lose hope, there is always tomorrow! Despite our downfalls, we must forgive ourselves and believe that one day we will feel worthy of nourishing ourselves with good food. It is only two words: being there! It is a very long journey.

It is difficult today to talk about food. We are so very different from each other. One thing, though, is common in all of us: our digestive system is in our stomach and intestines. Except, that is, the people who have moved it into their head, by following faddy popular diets or worrying or even obsessing about what they eat. Over-thinking about food is often the outcome of awareness that does not stop. This is an unhealthy, widespread phenomenon that cannot lead to nourishment, no matter how healthy the food we eat is. If you are stuck in your head about food, you should find a way to free yourself from this terrifying prison. Bring awareness to your diet, observe your reaction to food, see what does you good and what makes you feel bad. But also teach yourself to let go, move food back to where it belongs (in your stomach) and remember that the number one rule with healthy eating is to enjoy it!

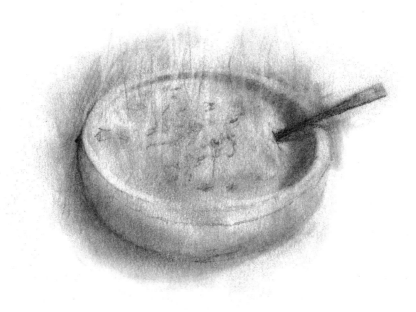

The composition of meals

Meals are the framework within which we feed ourselves and our families. In this book you will find meals for every day, and more festive meals for special events and times.

Some of the meals are complex, consisting of soup, a main dish, salad and dessert and some are more simple, consisting of a rich soup which is itself the main dish. The choice and the creativity are in your hands. Listed below are some guidelines for the composition of meals:

1. In every meal it is desirable to have a representative of each different part of the plant: root, leaf, flower, fruit and seed.
   For example:
   Roots: carrot, radish, beetroot (beet), parsley root, celeriac and others.
   Leaves: lettuce, celery leaves, parsley, dill, leek, onion, garlic, green cabbage and red cabbage, fresh coriander (cilantro), spinach, Swiss chard and others.
   Flowers: cauliflower, broccoli, herb teas (hibiscus, chamomile, elderflower).
   Fruits: tomato, cucumber, courgette (zucchini), aubergine (eggplant) and peppers, and fruits of trees (apple, peach, citrus fruit and others), and fruits of the forest (blackberry, strawberry, raspberry and others).
   Seeds: all grains (see the chapter about them), all pulses (beans, lentils, dry and fresh peas), sesame seeds, spices (black pepper, cumin, cardamom, caraway, coriander, mustard) and others.

2. A variety of colours means a nourishing abundance and diversity. Integrate differently coloured components into your meals.

3. Every meal must contain a grain.

4. If you add dairy products to your soup, the rest of the meal should be non-dairy. Or if the main dish is dairy, serve a non-dairy dessert.

In short, go slow with dairy. If you are altogether allergic to it, find recipes that are dairy-free rather than replacing the milk products with your invention (my customers have told me about using tofu or flaxseed crushed and mixed with water), or I cannot be responsible for the outcome!

5. Diversify tastes but keep a balance between flavours! If the main dish is sweet, there is no need for a dessert. A balance between the basic tastes of bitter, salty, sweet, sour and oily (fatty, like recipes rich in nuts) is an absolute necessity. I have made a great effort to show, through my recipes, how to do this. I recommend you start by following the recipes! After you have mastered harmony in tastes, you can create your own recipes and menus.

6. Balance quantities. If the meal has many components, eat a little of each thing. If the meal is simple and consists of only one or two components, you can eat more.

7. When you prepare a meal for a large number of people, pay attention to the amount of food that you prepare. There is no need to calculate a serving for each person. Instead, the variety of the dishes should widen. If there are, for example, fifteen people at your dinner and you make a soup, you can double the vegetable pie, make three salads and one cake, and have a satisfying meal. You will learn from your mistakes. Besides, it is always possible to eat the leftovers over following days.

Replacing sugar and flour

Agave nectar can be used to replace sugar if you do not wish to eat sugar, though it is considerably more expensive. It is sweeter than sugar so reduce the quantity. It is purchased as a liquid, so you will also need to slightly reduce liquids in the recipe.

Flour (wheat) can be replaced in some recipes with oatbran (very yummy but it still has gluten in it) or chickpea flour (this has a powerful taste, so it is alright for savoury dishes, but not in cakes!).

The kitchen: the heart of the home

The kitchen is the heart of the home. It is the centre of the family, and more time is spent there than in any other space in the house. Even children who hide in their rooms with a computer or television will eventually emerge to arrive at the refrigerator.

A warm house, in the full meaning of the term, depends not only on the parent's heart but also on the kitchen. Cooking with delicious smells that activate the digestive juices and invite everyone to come to the kitchen and ask, 'What are we eating today?' are a meeting point for the whole family. In my cooking courses I gather the participants into a circle and ask them to close their eyes and return with the eyes of their spirit to the kitchen where they grew up. I ask them to describe it physically (its size and its position in the house) and also to describe its spirit and soul. (Were there stimulating smells? Was there a mother with a wide heart or a stingy one? Was she strict or relaxed? Was she aware of healthy food or not? Was her taste interesting or conventional and boring?) Usually, the kitchen stories that people tell 'from the stomach' are very touching: sometimes sad and depressing and sometimes heartwarming and humourous. Some people burst into tears, either because remembering the bad food they were given is painful forever or the opposite: remembering granny's delicious food and cakes causes them to miss her!

Memories that are connected to food are important for our biography. Food is central to our lives and the activity of eating is almost the first one we learn when we arrive into this world.

A kitchen needs to be full of heartwarming objects that will satisfy you when you are around them: beautiful utensils (made from ceramic, enamel, glass, clay and wood) and iron or stainless steel pots. Flowers

and plants will fill your kitchen with life and colour. Avoid sterility in the space where Life is created, such as too many machines, stainless steel surfaces or too many plastic objects. My absolute greatest fear from the health authority's visit is that she will order me to get a stainless steel table instead of the big beautiful wooden table that Muafak (our Arab neighbour) built thirty years ago. It has nothing wrong with it except that in an office in a ministry, a bureaucrat has decided that it is not sterile enough for businesses. You can probably imagine my views on health regulations!

A few years ago I renovated my house and moved the old kitchen, which was facing a wall. The new kitchen is made mostly of windows: on one side I see the sea, on the other I see the most northern mountains of Lebanon. My kitchen windows bring the beautiful nature views in, so no wonder I love to spend every free moment there (I wrote this book sitting at my kitchen table, in front of the windows).

It does not matter what kitchen you had in your childhood; try to create a warm, beautiful, simple kitchen for yourself now, where you will be happy to spend a large part of your day.

Recommended ingredients

The aim of this book is to inspire you to cook tasty and healthy food, which will nourish you. Cooking also needs to be an enjoyable experience, free from feelings of blame or fear. I do not demand in every recipe that you use organic or biodynamic produce. Rather this is my general recommendation. Biodynamic food is enhanced with life forces, which are impossible to compare to any other substance. They are almost not substance, as they are so highly connected to spirit. This is the best! Organic food is good. Non-organically grown food should be consumed only if you can't find or afford the others.

This is a meeting between you and I, wherein I suggest and you choose each moment what suits you. Biodynamic or organic food is an ideal that seems very distant to most people. Do not feel guilty if you are still not 'there'. Guilt can't be a guest in the space where you cook!

The following list gives my recommendations for ingredients to create a healthy, nourishing kitchen.

Biodynamic or organic ingredients for cooking:

Fruit and vegetables

Wholewheat flour or spelt flour (These can be substituted one for another in all recipes.)

Whole grains (See the chapter on the seven grains.)

Dairy products (Goat or sheep milk dairy products are advisable, but I am not against cow's milk products.)

Eggs (Eggs must be organic.)

Tofu (Find tofu made from non-genetically engineered soy beans.)

Legumes (White and red beans, lentils, peas, mung beans.)

Vinegar (We use apple cider vinegar and balsamic vinegar.)

Soy sauce (We use an organic soy sauce, which does not contain wheat.)

Coconut milk (This has become very popular, as it can replace milk or cream. Unfortunately, most coconut milks are full of preservatives, so look for one that has the least!)

Chickpea flour can replace any type of flour in savoury dishes if you need to be gluten free.

It is advisable to avoid or consume as little as possible:

Yeast

Baking powder (Baking powder accelerates the baking process and
continues to be active inside our bodies as an accelerating agent
and a stimulant.)

It is advisable to avoid completely:

Processed and ready-made food (During processing, life forces are
destroyed.)

Canned vegetables (Life forces cannot be canned. There is no life in
what is found inside the can.)

Frozen food (Frozen food is one level above canned food, but I would
not use frozen food on a daily basis, only in emergency situations.)

White sugar (Read more about balancing our sugar consumption in
the chapter entitled 'Home-made biscuits, cookies, slices'.)

Use of the microwave (Read more about its use in the section 'Cooking
and the digestive system'.)

The household budget is a matter of priorities. If you invest in organic food,
you may need to give up other things. If the family budget is restricted, it
is advisable to start the shift to organic with basic products – bread, dairy
products and eggs – and only later to include fruits and vegetables.

Basic Recipes, Techniques and Secrets

The secret of the fresh salad

Hungarians do not have a culture of eating fresh salad such as exists in Israel. In this area I have a lot to learn. I am still amazed by the amount of salad that Israelis can eat. It does not matter how many fresh vegetables are on the table, they will be finished in no time. Hungarians are more fond of pickles and prefer pickled cucumber, peppers (bell peppers) stuffed with red cabbage and a pickled vegetable mix called *csalamádé*, which has white cabbage, cucumber, carrot, cauliflower and pepper (bell pepper) in the same jar. The farmer's market in the city where I grew up explodes with activity in summer time and is almost empty in winter, because the farmers are dependent on the weather and the limited number of vegetables that grow get frozen while they are standing in the covered but unheated market. My family spent the summer months preparing all kinds of pickles in jars, which stood in long rows on the pantry shelves.

Thirty years in Israel has taught me to love salad, and it has even become one of the things that I most want to eat. However, my creativity with food is still not expressed in salad. That is the reason why, in my book, you will find only simple salads.

I love waiting a few months for a particular vegetable, until its season arrives. Then, when I taste its flavour, it is a real festival. There is no comparison between a tomato that has ripened in summer time, red and with a wonderful smell, and the pallid, flavourless and scentless tomato of the winter months. If you cook according to the seasons you will not only be a part of the cycle of the earth's breath, but your creativity will grow from the need to invent different recipes from the same vegetables.

56

'What shall I cook today, when there are only leaves and roots?' you ask in November, and the earth and the sky will help you to find the right dish.

Basic salad

The basis of every good salad is leaves: lettuce of every kind (regular, curly, red) and other leaves (rocket [arugula], baby spinach, mustard leaves and others). In a large bowl filled with water, wash the leaves. It is desirable to dry them in a kitchen towel or to leave them to dry for a number of hours in a colander. After drying, start the preparation of the salad.

1. It is best to tear the leaves by hand, but sometimes they are too hard and it is necessary to use a knife. Recently I have obtained a ceramic knife that is extremely sharp but very good for cutting leaves. Now mix the leaves, preferably in a wooden bowl.
2. Add other vegetables, chopped or grated: carrot, tomato, cucumber, red pepper (bell pepper), cauliflower, red cabbage, white cabbage, radish, cooked or uncooked grated beetroot (beet).
3. It is possible to add fresh chopped herbs such as basil, thyme (a little), parsley, dill, oregano, marjoram, coriander (cilantro), chives or spring onion (scallions). Use herbs cautiously because they have strong flavours, which can be overpowering. It is preferable to choose just one herb.
4. Add lemon juice or vinegar and oil. Add lemon juice before olive oil, as the oil prevents the absorption of any other ingredients. (The ratio of oil to vinegar or lemon is three spoons of oil to one spoon of vinegar. It is possible to add a higher ratio of lemon.)
5. It is possible to substitute other salad dressings (recipes will follow) for lemon or vinegar and oil.
6. Other additions: boiled egg, bean sprouts (see page 64), croutons (see page 84), sunflower seeds (see page 85), sesame and salt (see page 78), toasted walnuts, pumpkin seeds, feta cheese, Roquefort cheese, red onion chopped into pieces and marinated in a glass jar in 6 spoons of olive oil and two spoons of vinegar, avocado and more... be creative!

Salad dressings

House dressing

If you have some left over, this will keep in a jar in the fridge for a few days.

100 ml (½ cup) mayonnaise (see page 60)
200 ml (1 cup) yogurt (see page 62)
4 tbs soy sauce
2 spring onions (scallions), chopped

Mix together.

Roquefort dressing

This is a very rich dressing so I would use it with a simple meal.

50 ml (¼ cup) mayonnaise (see page 60)
150 ml (¾ cup) yogurt (see page 62)
30 g (¼ cup) Roquefort cheese, grated
100 ml (½ cup) honey (optional)
a pinch of black pepper

Mix together.

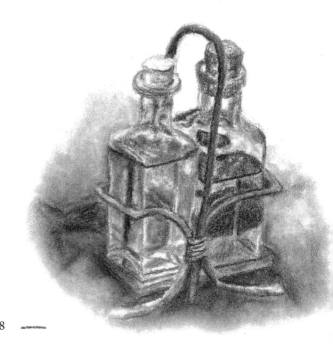

French dressing (V)

A large quantity, but it keeps for months in the refrigerator.

180 ml (¾ cup) sunflower oil
180 ml (¾ cup) olive oil
60 ml (¼ cup) apple vinegar
3 tbs apple juice concentrate
3 garlic cloves, crushed
½ tbs smooth Dijon mustard
2 tbs soy sauce
salt and black pepper to taste

Mix together in a food processor or blender.

Sesame dressing (V)

1 tbs sesame oil
5 tbs olive oil
3 tbs lemon juice
1 tbs soy sauce
1 garlic clove, crushed
½ tbs honey (optional)

Mix together.

Mayonnaise

Mayonnaise can be used as a wonderful spread for sandwiches or as a base for house dressing or Roquefort dressing. It keeps for one week in the refrigerator.

Makes about 480 ml (2 cups)

1 egg
1 tsp salt
black pepper
1 ½ tbs Dijon mustard
3 garlic cloves, crushed (optional)
half a bunch parsley, chopped
1 ½ tbs vinegar or lemon
360 ml (1 ½ cups) sunflower oil

Blend all the ingredients apart from the oil in a food processor. Add the oil slowly in a small stream. Stop the food processor as the mayonnaise begins to harden.

Green mayonnaise

half a bunch parsley, chopped
half a bunch chives, chopped or spring onion (scallions), chopped

Add the parsley to the basic mayonnaise in the food processor. After you have finished with the food processor, stir in the chives or spring onions (scallions).

Sesame mayonnaise

300 ml (1 ¼ cups) sunflower oil
60 ml (¼ cup) sesame oil

Follow the regular mayonnaise recipe but use this mix of sunflower oil and sesame oil instead of just sunflower oil.

The secret of good soup: good stock!

I suggest you purchase an electric hand blender for turning the vegetables into purée for soup. Otherwise, you can transfer all of the soup to a regular blender or food processor and then return it to the pot, but this creates a lot of chaos and washing up!

Preparing the vegetable stock for the soup

Most recipes for soups and stews recommend using stock. Stock is the secret of a good soup! At the Harduf restaurant we take stock very seriously. It is an old method of cooking soup that was common before the age of bouillon powder and stock cubes, which does not enter our kitchen (not even the organic kinds). The use of bouillon or stock cubes makes everything taste the same, and there is no longer a challenge to find the perfect herb or spice for each dish.

Preparing stock is also ecological, because we do not waste the pieces of vegetables that are usually thrown away. We use vegetables that are already 'tired' of their life and vegetable scraps (peels, stems, seeds and tips) that would have been thrown away.

When we clean the vegetables (preferably in a large bowl and not under a running tap, it is a pity to waste a single drop!) we put the scraps in a large pot (and if we are not making it straight away, they can be kept in a plastic bowl in the fridge): green leek leaves (to my great horror most people simply throw away this part of the leek); carrot and courgette (zucchini) tips; broccoli and cauliflower leaves and stems; dill, parsley and coriander (cilantro) stems; kohlrabi, sweet potato, pumpkin and butternut peels; tired leaves of spinach, chives, celery and white cabbage; off-cuts of green or yellow beans. There are a few vegetables – like red cabbage, aubergine (eggplant) and beetroot (beet) – that it is preferable not to add to the stock because they have a dominant or bitter flavour and strong, unwanted colour.

Cover the vegetable scraps with water, bring to the boil and cook for at least half an hour, strain them (throw the vegetables into the compost) and now you have a fabulous stock for preparing soups, stews or sauces. It is possible to freeze the stock and use as needed.

Ricotta cheese

Home-made ricotta cheese is tastier and cheaper than the supermarket one (unless you live in Italy).

Makes 700–750 g (1 1/2 lb)

5 litres (10 ½ U.S. pints) milk
7–8 tbs apple vinegar or lemon juice

1. Prepare a sieve (strainer), inlaid with a thin cloth (like a new nappy or diaper cloth).
2. Boil the milk in a pot.
3. Add the vinegar or the lemon juice and keep boiling for 2–3 minutes, until the liquids and the non-liquids separate. Take off the heat.
4. Pour into the sieve with the cloth and let the liquid drip through into another pot. It is possible to put a weight on the cloth.
5. If you want hardened ricotta, leave it for a whole day in the cloth.

Yogurt

Makes about 1 kg (2 lb)

Boil 1 litre (2 U.S. pints) milk. Cool until the milk reaches 39° C (102° F) or until it is cool enough to put your finger in it and not get burned. It is important that the milk doesn't get too cold. If it does (which happened to me many times) you can heat the milk again.

Add 3 tbs live biotic yogurt and mix thoroughly.

Cover the pot and wrap it in a cloth or towel. Leave for 5 hours at room temperature, than put it in the refrigerator.

Actually, it works best if you put the pot under your blanket. (Maybe instead of a lover?)

Our labane

This is a soft white cheese made from yogurt that is popular in the Mediterranean and the Middle East.

You will need at least 2 litres (4 U.S. pints) of yogurt for making the labane.

1. Line a sieve (strainer) with a cloth and put the sieve into a pot.
2. Pour the yogurt into the sieve and cover with the remaining edges of the cloth. Leave for a day until the liquids drip through. It is important not to let the yogurt in the cloth touch the liquid below. Some people hang the cloth from the tap and then the liquid just drips down into a bowl underneath.
3. After a day the strained yogurt is labane, and is ready for eating.

I recommend serving this with olive oil and *zatar*. (This is a Middle-Eastern herb mixture, mostly made by Bedouin women. It is based on hyssop and sesame seeds. You might be able to find it at Middle-Eastern stores.)

In the restaurant at Harduf, we make spreads with labane using garlic and dill or *korozott* (a Hungarian spread with sweet paprika, caraway seeds and spring onion or scallion).

I drink the remaining liquid whey that drips from the labane – to the amazement of the kitchen staff! This liquid contains minerals and vitamins. It can also be used to make stock for a sour soup.

Germinating pulses or seeds

There are hard pulses (all the different kinds of bean, chick pea and soya) and there are soft ones (all the different kinds of lentil, mung bean and dry pea). The hard beans have to be soaked in water before cooking overnight, and the soft ones don't. To get the most nourishment from them, though, it is recommended to germinate them. The dry seeds are dormant and can keep that way for a long time. When germinated, they 'wake up' to life and whoever eats them gets the nourishing life forces that are released.

I use mung beans because they never let me down!

1. Soak the mung beans overnight using three times more water than beans.
2. Drain and pour out the water. Don't reuse the water, as it contains all the poison extracted from the beans.

For cooking:

3. To sprout for cooking, leave the beans in a sieve for 24 hours. Wet them occasionally. Then use them for cooking. In this process, the beans start to soften.

OR **for salad:**

3. To make bean sprouts for salad, keep wetting the beans in the sieve for a few days (we do it once a day) until a short white leaf appears. The speed of the process depends on the temperature. Sometimes two or more days are needed. The easiest pulse to germinate is mung bean.

Menus Through the Week: The seven grains

The seven grains

Grains are an important part of human nutrition. They are connected to our nervous system, and therefore also to consciousness and wisdom, but they also nourish the metabolic and rhythmic system and contain all the food groups that we need: protein, carbohydrate, fat and minerals.

All grains are seeds. The cycle of a plant's life includes the seed in the earth, the sprout, the leaf, the flower, the fruit and the seeds in the fruit. The seed contains, in its compact form, everything that is needed to build the next plant. The creation of seeds is the climax and the end of the plant's life cycle. Because they carry within them all the forces of the cosmos (earth, air, water, warmth and the influence of the planets), seeds are very rich in energy.

Seeds have important functions: through them the plant multiplies; they are food to human beings and animals; and they contain oils, which have many uses, from food products to soap and paints.

All grains are seeds of a plant, but not all edible seeds are defined as grains; for example, beans, lentils, peas, quinoa and buckwheat are seeds but not grains.

We now know many different types of grains, including seven principal grains that were depended upon in the past and remain central in human nourishment today: wheat, rice, millet, corn, rye, oats and barley. According to an old legend, in their flight from Atlantis, before the big flood that covered it with water, the people of that ancient continent took their seven grains to different parts of the world: corn to America, millet to Africa, oats to the northern countries, rice to the East, rye to central and eastern Russia, and barley and wheat to Europe. This legend contains within it the connections, which were known in past cultures, between the seven grains and different parts of the world.

The seven days of the week are connected to seven planets, as their ancient Latin names suggest. Similarly, each grain has a connection to a planet. Out of this knowledge, a system of nourishment was created, based on eating a different grain every day of the week.

Eating grains according to days of the week is an almost impossible mission in the fast pace of modern life. However, it is the ideal, and we can hold it as a goal to aim for. In places that consider food as medicine, such as anthroposophical hospitals, and in caring for people with special needs, these guidelines are strictly followed. I personally try to eat as many types of grain as possible. I do not always manage to do it according to the correct order of the days.

Pay attention to which grain you tend to use more than others – usually this is wheat (bread, bulgar or cracked wheat, couscous, semolina) or rice. The grains of the week will help you to diversify your nutrition and unite with the whole world.

Some useful things to know about...

Rice

Each kind of rice has a different nutritional and culinary value. The most common kinds used are round rice, long rice, basmati rice, wild rice (which is not really a rice but an aquatic grass), sweet rice (also known as sticky rice mostly used in East Asian cuisines) and white rice. Round rice is stickier and chewier than long rice, which is fluffier – and more popular for this reason. I personally prefer round rice, also for its taste and for its higher nutritional value than long rice. In order to get more nutrients you can mix different kinds!

Millet

It is possible to improve the taste of millet by adding sautéd onion and garlic to it. It is possible to add a few drops of tamari (a kind of soy sauce) as well.

Buckwheat

Buckwheat is a very healthy seed. It revitalises our blood system, lowers blood pressure and cleanses our veins. I advise you to introduce it to your regular menu.

Cooking grains and seeds

GRAIN	SERVES	INGREDIENTS	DIRECTIONS
Brown rice	4–6	200 g (1 cup) brown rice 480 ml (2 cups) water ½ tsp salt	Boil, lower the heat and simmer for 1 hour with the lid on.
Rice mixture	8–12	300 g (1 ½ cups) round brown rice 50 g (¼ cup) red rice 50 g (¼ cup) round black rice or wild rice 1 litre (4 cups) water ½ tsp salt	Boil, lower the heat and simmer for 1 hour with the lid on.
Barley	4–6	200 g (1 cup) barley 480 ml (2 cups) water ¼ tsp salt	Boil, lower the heat and simmer for 1 hour with the lid on.
Millet	4–6	200 g (1 cup) millet 420 ml (1 ¾) cups boiling water 2 tsp fresh sage, chopped (optional) ½ tsp salt	Roast millet in the oven at 150° C (300° F) until golden. Move to pot and add the water, sage and salt. Simmer on low heat for 30–40 minutes. Add more water if needed.
Oat groats	4–6	200 g (1 cup) oat groats 420 ml (1 ¾) cups boiling water ¼ tsp salt (optional)	Simmer for 1 hour in a closed pot, on low heat. Add more water if needed. The cooked oats are not separated like rice; they are wet and rather sticky.

GRAIN	SERVES	INGREDIENTS	DIRECTIONS
Rye	4–6	200 g (1 cup) rye 480 ml (2 cups) water Another 60 ml (¼ cup) water ½ tsp salt	Boil the rye in 2 cups of water, take off the heat and cover with a lid. Wrap the pot in a cloth towel and leave overnight. Add 60 ml (¼ cup) water and the salt. Cover the pot and cook 20 minutes on low heat, until the seeds are soft.
Quinoa seed	4–6	175 g (1 cup) quinoa 360 ml (1 ½) cups boiling water ¼ tsp salt	Simmer for 30–40 minutes on low heat in a closed pot. Add water if needed.
Buckwheat seed	4–6	200 g (1 cup) buckwheat 480 ml (2 cups) water ½ tsp salt	Simmer for 30–40 minutes in a closed pot on low heat. Add water if needed.
Spelt	4–6	200 g (1 cup) spelt 480 ml (2 cups) water ½ tsp salt	Soak overnight, strain. Simmer in the 2 cups of water for 1 hour in a closed pot on a low heat. Add water if needed.
Cornmeal (*mamaliga*, polenta)	4–6	130 g (¾ cup) cornmeal 480 ml (2 cups) milk 120 ml (½ cup) water ¼ tsp salt	Boil the water and milk, then lower the heat. Add the cornmeal while stirring and cook for 5–10 minutes. Add the salt.

Improving the taste of grains (V)

Here is a simple recipe you can add to any cooked grain:

olive oil for sautéing
1 medium onion, finely chopped
1 medium carrot, grated
1 celery stalk, finely sliced

Sauté the onion in olive oil until golden. Add the carrot and celery, sauté for 10 more minutes.

Mix this into any cooked grain. With buckwheat, for example, the delicious taste will make you forget the not-so-pleasant smell of the buckwheat.

A note for health freaks: in order to fully waken the life forces of grains, we should soak them for a night. My recipes use unsoaked grains, for I believe in hectic modern life, most of us forget to soak. I myself eat unsoaked grains.

Mixed grains (V)

Keeps for 5 days refrigerated.

Makes 7 cups (cooked)

2 onions, chopped
olive oil for frying
½ tsp cardamom seeds, ground
¼ tsp nutmeg, grated
¼ tsp cumin seeds, ground
¼ tsp coriander seeds

> Fry the onions in oil until golden.
> Add the spices, fry and stir, for 2 more minutes.

1 tsp turmeric
100 g (½ cup) brown rice
100 g (½ cup) oat groats
100 g (½ cup) barley
1 litre (4 cups) boiling water
1 tsp salt (or to taste)

> Add, cover the pot and let it cook on a low heat for 20 minutes.

50 g (¼ cup) millet
40 g (¼ cup) quinoa

> Add and stir. Cover the pot, cook for 40 minutes more.

For me, this grain stew is a basic meal. It is always in the fridge and I eat it in the morning, afternoon and evening with salad, stir-fry or cooked vegetables.

WHEAT

Sunday, ☉ *Sun — Sol, dies Solis*

Sunday, as the name suggests, is connected to the sun, which is the centre around which our living planet moves. The planets, including the Earth on which we live, rotate around the sun whose force of gravity holds them in their path.

Sunday's grain is wheat, which needs the sun to ripen and turn golden. Wheat grows in summertime in every part of the world. The amount of sun that the grain receives differs from country to country and therefore there are differences in the quality of the wheat flour. The more sun the wheat absorbs, the harder the seed becomes and the higher the amount of gluten it contains. Hard wheat has the properties of glue; it is a uniting material. It is good to use it for baking bread and pastries. Gluten is also the component of wheat to which many people have a sensitivity, and even an allergy in the case of celiacs. Spelt is a good substitute for people who find eating wheat problematic, but for celiacs other flour types should be used, especially rice flour.

The light and warmth of the sun are essential for life processes. They nourish and activate life. The sun is the 'I' of the world, holding it all together, harmonising all activities, feelings and thoughts. People look for the sun just as plants look for light.

We usually eat too many wheat products, often without noticing. Wheat flour is found in pastries, bread, pies and cakes; couscous, bulgar and pastas are also made from wheat. It is advisable to diversify your grain consumption. It is, for example, possible to buy pastas made from different grains!

Sunday menu

HUNGARIAN TOMATO SOUP (v)

MUJADDARA WITH BULGAR (v)

BROCCOLI OR CAULIFLOWER SALAD (v)

**SALAD WITH OLIVE OIL
(SEE PAGE 57)**

DATE AND TAHINI PARFÉ (v)

Sunday in Israel is the first working day of the week,
so this is not a festive meal.

Hungarian tomato soup (V)

My grandmother often cooked this light soup in summertime, because tomatoes grew in abundance in our garden and we needed to use them. The soup is suitable for summer tomatoes, because they are the ripest and sweetest. My grandmother thickened the soup with roux; I prefer it without. I often think about the changes food cultures go through in one generation. As a child I loved this soup as it was served, with the roux. (Children were less fussy than today's kids.) But now I do not want either the fat of the roux or its flour in my soup.

Serves 6–8

1 kg fresh tomatoes
1 litre (4 cups) water

Cut the tomatoes in two. Cut out the white bottom part. Boil the water and throw in the tomatoes until their peel can easily be removed (about 8–10 minutes). Remove the peel and put the tomatoes back into the water.

2 large sticks celery (with the leaves)
1 large onion, cut into quarters
5 cloves of garlic

Add the chunky celery, onion and garlic to the tomatoes and cook for 20 minutes. Then take out the celery stalks, the onion chunks and the garlic cloves. Blend the tomatoes and the liquid with a hand blender.

4 tbs brown sugar
salt and pepper to taste

Add the sugar, salt and pepper to the soup and boil for 2–3 minutes. Serve with chopped fresh parsley or basil.

chopped fresh parsley or basil for garnish

You can add dumplings to this soup (see page 161). My grandmother always added them and we all loved this dish, partly because of the dumplings and partly because it was a light summer soup, which meant that there would be dessert that day as well.

The tomato – a little demon

The tomato belongs to a family of plants called nightshades. Peppers, aubergines (eggplants), potatoes and tobacco also belong to this family. Nightshades are regarded as mildly poisonous foods that are edible but can also cause harm. It is important to recognise this fact and understand that these plants should be used with moderation.

The poisonous material in nightshades is concentrated in the green part of the fruit that we eat (from a botanical perspective tomatoes, aubergines (eggplants) and peppers are fruits).

For this reason it is better not to use green peppers, and to cut off the light green part on the top of tomatoes and the green bits that sometimes occur on potatoes. Some approaches to nutrition avoid eating nightshades; my approach is that you can eat them but not too often and definitely only one kind in any one meal.

It's interesting to note that Mediterranean countries' menus and eating habits are heavily based on nightshades. If I go to an Arab restaurant (which I do), I will get on the table: aubergine (eggplant) salad, cherry-tomato salad, peppers (bell peppers) baked in the oven and, of course, potato chips. Next to these, though, there will be a tabbouleh, green leaves, hummus, tahini, cucumber salad and many more surprises.

Continues

When I prepare a meal with a recipe containing a large quantity of tomatoes (such as pasta, pizza or lasagna), the salad will definitely not include any vegetable from the nightshade family. You can also be sensitive to your digestive system. If you habitually eat healthy food, it will tell you everything that you need to know. When I was younger, aubergines (eggplants) caused a strong physical reaction in my body. After I stopped eating them for a number of years, the reaction stopped completely. Perhaps growing old and eating a lot of good food gave my digestive system a better ability to cope with these demons and others like them.

Besides, without demons, life in this world would be boring!

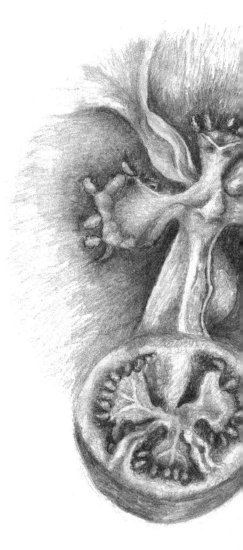

Mujaddara with bulgar (V)

I recommend sprouting all of the pulses (see page 64), and therefore I suggest starting the preparation of this *mujaddara* two days before you cook it. If you forget to sprout, you can still go ahead and make this simple but extremely delicious dish. The result is just as great. But most lentils like being soaked, even if it's only for a few hours.

Serves 4–5

olive oil for sautéing
3 medium onions, finely sliced
100 g (½ cup) lentils (brown, black or green), soaked for 6 hours or sprouted
200 g (1 cup) rough bulgar
¼ tsp cumin powder
salt and pepper
720 ml (3 cups) of boiling water
4 cloves of garlic, crushed

1. Sauté one of the sliced onions in olive oil until golden. Add the lentils, bulgar, cumin, salt and pepper. Stir. Add the water and cook for half an hour on a low heat until the lentils are soft.
2. Meanwhile, sauté the remaining two onions in olive oil until golden. Add the garlic and stir for one more minute.
3. Add the onion and garlic to the soft bulgar and lentil mixture and stir.

Instead of the bulgar, you can use brown rice, buckwheat, barley or a mix to your taste. Remember that the cooking time for harder grains is longer! (For the quantity of water other grains need, see page 68.)

Broccoli or cauliflower salad (V)

Serves 6–8

500 g broccoli or cauliflower – only the florets
80 g (½ cup) sesame seeds
salt to taste

Sesame sauce

1 tbs sesame oil
5 tbs olive oil
3 tbs lemon juice
1 tbs soy sauce
1 clove of garlic, crushed
½ tbs honey (optional)

1. Steam the broccoli or cauliflower for approximately 15 minutes in a pot with a little water in it. I suggest not over-steaming the florets: let them stay crispy and let the broccoli keep its fresh deep-green colour. Cool the florets and place them in a bowl.
2. Toast the sesame seeds and the salt in a frying pan or skillet on a low heat for 10 minutes, without any oil, stirring constantly. If you have a mortar, crush the toasted sesame and salt mixture into a rough powder. If you do not have one, just use the seeds as they are this time and ask someone to buy you a pestle and mortar for your birthday. Set aside.
3. Mix together the ingredients for the sauce.
4. Pour the sauce over the broccoli and sprinkle the sesame and salt mixture on top.

 ## Date and tahini parfé (V)

As a Hungarian who would dedicate hours to preparing a good dessert, I was surprised by this simple and delicious recipe that I learned from my cooking class partner. It is very rich in taste, texture and nutrition, so I suggest small portions!

You need to make this dish the day before you are going to serve it. It can stay in the freezer as long as you wish.

Serves 8

120 ml (½ cup) coconut milk (look for one that does not have loads of additives)

230 g (1 cup) tahini (this is a sesame seed paste; you can buy it in Middle-Eastern stores)

75 g (½ cup) crushed dates (sometimes there are nice additive-free date spreads!)

3 tbs honey (optional)

Mix together in a blender or food processor. Pour the mixture into the holes of a small muffin pan and freeze for one day before serving.

RICE

Monday, ☾ Moon – Luna, dies Lunae

The name of Monday in many languages of the world points to its connection to the moon (for example, *chandra* in Hindi, *lunedi* in Italian). After the sunny Sunday, Monday is moony: introspective, absorbed and reflective.

The grain related to this day is rice, which grows in water. The moon influences the movement of water over the earth. Rice has a weak root system and draws almost no substances for its nourishment from the earth. Thus it does not contain many minerals. As described earlier in 'Humans as upside-down plants' (see page 37) plant roots support our most mineral part, our head. As a result of rice having a very weak root, it gives almost no nourishment to the nerve–sense system of human beings (the head with its thinking quality). Rice awakens the systems of liquids in our bodies: it helps heal problems with the flow of liquids, like high blood pressure, weak kidneys or the accumulation of phlegm.

According to the anthroposophical viewpoint, there are four human temperaments: phlegmatic, sanguine, melancholic and choleric. The moon and rice belong to the watery phlegmatic temperament, which goes with the flow, and can adapt to and accept any situation.

Rice is the grain of the East – India, China, Thailand and Japan – and the qualities that it brings are associated with the East: inner contemplation, meditation and tranquility.

Monday menu

**ROUND BROWN RICE
(SEE PAGE 67)**

MEDITERRANEAN VEGETABLE STEW (V)

BAKED FENNEL (V)

**HOUSE SALAD WITH CROUTONS
AND TOASTED SUNFLOWER SEEDS**

CARROT CAKE

Mediterranean vegetable stew (V)

I suggest serving this stew with brown rice, or pasta made from brown flour. Children tend to like it. If they are fussy and don't want to eat vegetables, you can blend the stew after it's cooked. In our restaurant this recipe, without the cauliflower, is the sauce for lasagne and moussaka.

Serves 6–8

2 big onions, chopped
olive oil for sautéing
half a garlic bulb, crushed
2 big carrots, sliced
1 red pepper (bell pepper), cut into strips
1 celery stick with its leaves, chopped
¼ cauliflower, broken into small florets

> Sauté the onions in the olive oil until golden. Add the garlic. Add the other vegetables and sauté for 2 more minutes.

1 tbs thyme
2 bay leaves
200 ml (1 cup) stock or water
2 tomatoes, chopped small

> Add and cook for 15 minutes.

½ cup tomato paste
1 cup fresh crushed tomatoes

> Add and cook for another 15 minutes.

salt and pepper to taste
¼ tbs hot paprika (optional)
2 tbs sugar

> Add and cook for half an hour, until the stew thickens a bit.

1 big courgette (zucchini), sliced
half a bunch parsley, chopped
4 tbs fresh basil, chopped
2 tbs fresh oregano, chopped, or 1 tbs dried oregano
3 tbs dry red wine (optional)

> Add after you have turned the heat off, stir, and cover the pot.

Baked fennel (V)

In order to allow the special taste of the fennel to be enjoyed, I add very few other flavours!

Serves 4–6

Preheat the oven to 180° C (350° F).

> 2 fennel bulbs, each cut lengthwise and then again crosswise (cut again if the bulbs are very large)
> 80 ml (⅓ cup) olive oil
> 4 cloves garlic, sliced
> 120 ml (½ cup) water

1. Place the fennel into a baking dish.
2. Mix the rest of the ingredients and pour on the fennel.
3. Bake. From time to time, pour some of the 'juice' over the fennel. Take out after 20 minutes or when a knife goes through the fennel easily.

House salad

Serves 8–10

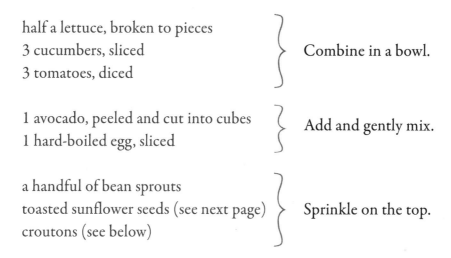

half a lettuce, broken to pieces
3 cucumbers, sliced
3 tomatoes, diced
}
Combine in a bowl.

1 avocado, peeled and cut into cubes
1 hard-boiled egg, sliced
}
Add and gently mix.

a handful of bean sprouts
toasted sunflower seeds (see next page)
croutons (see below)
}
Sprinkle on the top.

Add the house dressing (see page 58) a minute before serving.

Home-made croutons (v)

1. Preheat oven to 180° C (350° F).
2. Cut bread (preferably wholewheat bread that has no pieces of seed or wholegrain in it) into cubes of the crouton size you desire. Place the cubes in a baking tin.
3. Mix olive oil or melted butter with crushed garlic, sesame seeds and finely chopped dill or dried marjoram. In Israel we use a herb mixture called *zatar* instead of the dried herbs above. You could try to find it in Middle Eastern stores.
4. Pour the oil and herb mixture on the bread cubes and, using your hands or a wooden spoon, turn until the oil and herbs cover all of the bread.
5. Bake for 20 minutes or until the cubes are golden. You must stir with a wooden spoon from time to time.

Toasted sunflower seeds (V)

These keep well for months without refrigeration and elevate every salad!

Preheat oven to 150° C (300° F).

200 g (1 cup) of sunflower seeds
2–3 tbs soy sauce

Mix seeds and sauce well. Roast for 20 minutes on a baking dish or tray, stirring from time to time. Cool, then store them in a jar.

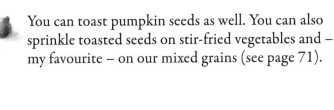 You can toast pumpkin seeds as well. You can also sprinkle toasted seeds on stir-fried vegetables and – my favourite – on our mixed grains (see page 71).

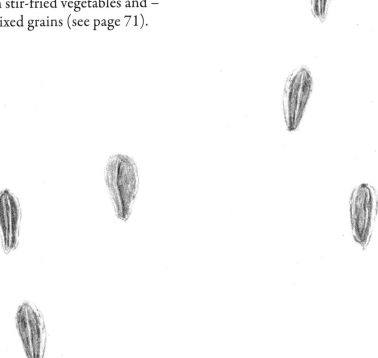

Carrot cake

Prepare a round, 28 cm (11 in) diameter cake tin or 2 loaf tins about 30 cm (12 in) in length.

Preheat the oven to 160° C (320° F).

4 eggs, beaten
180 ml (¾ cup) sunflower oil
200 g (1 cup) brown sugar
1 tbs honey
½ tbs cinnamon
1 tsp bicarbonate (baking) soda
2 tsp vanilla essence (extract) (good quality!)

} Mix in a bowl.

300 g (2 cups) wholewheat flour
75 g (½ cup) raisins
30 g (¼ cup) walnuts or pecan nuts, chopped

} Mix in a separate bowl. Add to the egg mixture and combine.

300 g (3 cups) of finely grated carrots
180 ml (¾ cup) of orange or apple juice

} Add and mix well.

Pour the cake mix into the prepared tin or tins.
   Bake for 75 minutes.

BARLEY

Tuesday, ♂ Mars – Mars, dies Martis

After the reflective, internal Monday, Tuesday arrives, full of vigour and activity. In Latin it is the day of Mars (*dies Martis*), who was the god of war.

The grain connected to this day is barley. Barley is rich in phosphorus, zinc, iron, magnesium and B vitamins. It is highly beneficial for muscle activity and for the function of the digestive system.

Eating barley strengthens general weaknesses, supports the heat processes in the body, and therefore assists with different kinds of inflammations.

The temperament connected to barley is choleric – which is hot, active and full of life.

Barley is the grain of Eastern Europe.

Some people connect oats with Tuesday and barley with Friday. You are free to choose. As far as I am concerned, the important thing is to vary your grain consumption!

Tuesday menu

WARMING WINTER SOUP WITH BARLEY (V)

BULGAR ROLLS SERVED WITH GIVETCH (V)
(A RICH TRANSYLVANIAN VEGETABLE SPREAD)

LABANE (SEE PAGE 63) WITH OLIVE OIL

REFRESHING SALAD (V)

HOME-MADE ICE CREAM

Warming winter soup with barley (V)

This soup is a perfect meal in itself since it contains a pulse, a grain and lots of vegetables. Note that the lentils need to be pre-soaked for an hour.

Serves 10 – 12

olive oil for sautéing
3 big onions, chopped into small pieces
1 leek, sliced
1 tbs caraway seed

} Sauté until golden.

2 litres (4 U.S. pints) stock or water
100 g (½ cup) red lentils (pre-soaked for 1hour)
100 g (½ cup) barley
¼ cauliflower, broken into florets
1 big carrot, sliced round
1 small sweet potato, cubed
1 medium potato, cubed
1 celeriac or parsley root, cubed
1 kohlrabi, roughly grated
2 celery stalks with the leaves, finely cut
½ tbs sweet paprika
1 bunch of dill or parsley, finely chopped
salt and pepper

} Add and cook for 40 minutes until the barley is soft.

lemon juice (optional)

When you serve, add a dash of lemon juice.

You can substitute dumplings (see page 161) for the barley. If you do, put them straight into the soup just before the end of the cooking time. Boil the soup for another 5–8 minutes, to cook the dumplings through.

Bulgar rolls (V)

Makes 15–20 rolls

200 g (1 cup) fine bulgar (there is a rough type too)
240 ml (1 cup) boiling water
4 tbs oil
4 tbs molasses or honey

Pour the water on the bulgar and mix. After half an hour add the molasses or honey and the oil. Cover with a kitchen towel and cool.

1 tbs dry or 25 g (1 oz) fresh yeast
240 ml (1 cup) lukewarm water
2 tbs molasses or honey
225 g (1 ½ cups) wholewheat flour
plus 450–600 g (3–4 cups) more wholewheat flour
melted butter for brushing on the rolls

1. Mix the yeast, water, molasses and 225 g (1 ½ cups) of flour in a big bowl. Cover with a kitchen towel and let it rise for 30–40 minutes.
2. Add the bulgar mixture and the extra flour. Knead well for a few minutes. If it needs still more flour, add more gradually until you get an elastic dough that does not stick to your hands but is not too dry either.
3. Let it rise again for half an hour.
4. Preheat oven to 180° C (350° F). Pull off a small piece of dough, form a roll, brush it with melted butter, let it rise again for 10 minutes, then sprinkle sesame or sunflower seeds, or rolled oats, on it.
5. Place the rolls onto a greased baking tray (sheet) and bake for 20–30 minutes.

Hungarian givetch (vegetable spread) (v)

This recipe is given in a large quantity, suitable for the sweet red pepper (bell pepper) season. Excess can be stored in sterilized jars or frozen in small containers to be used all year round. Of course it is also possible to prepare only a quarter of the quantity specified, store it in a container in the refrigerator and use it within a month. *Givetch* tastes good on sandwiches with feta cheese, garlic-dill cheese or omelette. I recommend you also add cucumber slices to the sandwich to counteract the spiciness of the *givetch*. Note that the beans need to be soaked for 2 days before the *givetch* is prepared.

Makes approximately two 500 g (1 lb) jars of givetch.

olive oil for sautéing
400 g (2 cups) dry white beans (or chickpeas)
3 medium onions, chopped
5 large red peppers (bell peppers), sliced
hot paprika or chilli (optional)
quarter bunch of celery, stalks and leaves, chopped
200 g (1 cup) passata (tomato purée)
salt and black pepper

 There are many varieties of *givetch*. For example, you can substitute courgette (zucchini) or peeled aubergine (eggplant) for some of the peppers (bell peppers).

1. Soak and sprout the beans for 2 days (see page 64). Put them in a cooking pot, cover well with water and cook for 2 hours until they are soft. Strain and cool.
2. Sauté the onions in plenty of olive oil until golden. Add the red pepper (bell pepper) and celery, then the hot paprika or chilli according to taste. Sauté until all the vegetables are soft.
3. Take the sautéd vegetables off the heat and put them into a food processor together with the beans. Blend them together until they turn into a paste.
4. Pour this paste back into the cooking pot, add the salt, pepper and the passata (tomato purée) and cook on a very low heat, stirring constantly with a wooden spoon. Take care not to burn the paste.

Refreshing salad (V)

Serves 8–10

quarter head of white cabbage, chopped finely
2 cucumbers, sliced
2 carrots, cut into matchsticks
half a red pepper (bell pepper), sliced finely
half a green pepper (bell pepper), sliced finely
2 tomatoes, chopped as you like
1 gherkin (pickled cucumber), sliced

Mix in a bowl.

5–8 tbs French dressing (see page 59)
or 5–8 tbs house dressing (see page 58)
fresh chopped basil

Pour on the salad and mix.

Home-made ice cream

I learnt this recipe from Suzanne Hillen, whose family I cooked for when I lived in Forest Row. In a way, she is the person responsible for me becoming a cookery teacher. As I was cooking in her gorgeous kitchen with its big Aga, its huge old wooden table, and her two year old, Rose, helping me with an apron on, she asked me to tell her about the deep meaning of food. I had been studying this subject with all the cooks of the area so I happily shared my understandings with her. One day she surprised me by saying, 'Why don't you give my friends a short cooking course?' Quite apprehensively I agreed – and enjoyed it so much that I am still doing it today, twenty years later.

This recipe amazes me with its simplicity. Also, it requires no special equipment, just a hand mixer. Once you eat this exquisite ice cream, you won't buy commercial ice cream ever again.

Makes 2 litres (4 U.S. pints)

4 eggs
50 g (¼ cup) and 100 g (½ cup) brown sugar
500 ml (1 U.S. pint) whipping cream
Your choice of flavouring from the list that follows this recipe.

1. Separate the eggs, keeping both yolks and whites.
2. Whip the egg yolks with 100 g (½ cup) of sugar and the desired flavouring from the list that follows this recipe.
3. Whip the cream.
4. Whip the egg whites with 50 g (¼ cup) of sugar. (There's no need to wash the mixer the whole way through making the ice cream!)
5. Fold the whipped egg white and the whipped cream into the flavoured yolk mix.
6. Pour the mix into a plastic box and freeze for at least 24 hours.

Ice cream flavour choices:

Carob: ½ tbs carob powder, sifted

Carob and tahini: 5 tbs carob powder plus 50 g (¼ cup) tahini

Chocolate: 3–4 tbs chocolate sauce (see page 123)

Cinnamon and honey: 3 tbs honey plus 1 tbs cinnamon (and use only
    100 g – ½ cup – of sugar in total in the base recipe)

Date and nut: 300 g (2 cups) crushed dates or date spread plus 60 g (½ cup) walnuts
    or pecans, toasted and chopped

Fig: 5 tbs fig jam

Fruit: any kind you wish, 500 g (1 lb)

Ginger: 3 tbs crystalised ginger, finely grated

Irish cream: 120 ml (½ cup) Irish cream liquor

Passion fruit: 100 g (½ cup) of passion fruit pulp

Rum and raisin: 100 g (4 oz) raisins or sultanas soaked for 1 night (minimum)
    in 4 tbs rum (real rum!)

Strawberry: 5 tbs strawberry jam or 500 g (1 lb) fresh strawberries, crushed

Vanilla: 1 tbs good quality vanilla essence (extract) or 1 tbs vanilla powder

For other amazing tastes, use your imagination!

MILLET

Wednesday, Mercury ☿ Mercurius, dies Mercurii

Wednesday is the day of Mercury, the messenger of the Gods, connected to healing and communication. In Latin-based languages the name of Wednesday is Mercurii, which is the closest planet to the sun.

Wednesday's grain is millet. It grows well in dry regions, almost without irrigation. The protein content of millet is similar to that in an omelette, but it is gluten-free and therefore is suitable for those who suffer from gluten allergies. It is rich in phosphorus, iron, calcium, vitamin B2, vitamin B3, lecithin and amino acids.

Millet primarily helps with preventing and healing allergies and skin problems.

Wednesday is the day of the active, sanguine temperament that jumps from one thing to another, not stopping to internally process and digest experiences.

Millet is the grain of Africa.

Wednesday menu

KASHMIR SPINACH (V)

MILLET SOUFFLÉ

EXOTIC CARROT SALAD (V)

INDIVIDUAL FRUIT TART

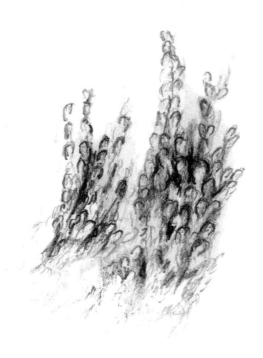

Kashmir spinach (V)

Serves 4–6

olive oil for sautéing
1 onion, chopped
1 kg spinach, washed, chopped
½ tbs turmeric
½ tbs chilli
salt
120 ml (½ cup) water
¼ tbs garam masala

1. In a large pan, sauté the onion in oil until transparent.
2. Add the spinach, turmeric, chilli and salt and sauté
   for 5 minutes.
3. Add the water. Bring to a boil, lower the heat and cook
   for 5–10 minutes until most of the water has evaporated.
4. Add the garam masala.

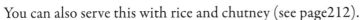

You can also serve this with rice and chutney (see page212).

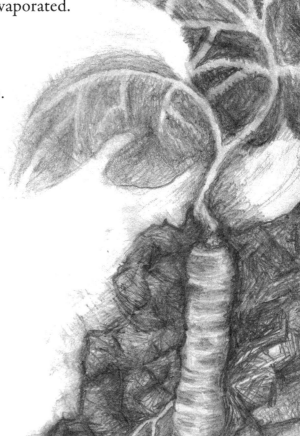

Millet soufflé

The soufflé rises like a cake and should be served immediately.

This dish requires a large baking dish or tin, 40 x 38 cm (15 x 14 in), or two round pie dishes.
   Preheat the oven to 150° C (300° F), and grease the baking dishes.

This recipe has four parts:

   the millet
   the vegetables
   the béchamel sauce
   the eggs

The millet

200 g (1 cup) millet } Toast in a dry, deep pan on medium heat for 10–15 minutes until it turns a light brown colour.

420 ml (1 ¾ cups) boiling water
1 tsp salt } Add to the millet. Cook on a low heat for 25 minutes with the lid on.

The vegetables

olive oil for sautéing
3 big leeks or 3 big onions, sliced finely } In a separate pan from the millet, sauté until golden, about 10 minutes.

4 cloves garlic, crushed
1 big carrot, roughly grated
2 celery stalks with leaves, finely chopped
other vegetables of your choice – for example,
    red peppers (bell peppers), cabbage,
    mushrooms – finely chopped, or thickly
    sliced for more 'bite' in the final texture

Add the rest of the vegetables to the leeks or onions and sauté another 5 minutes.

The béchamel sauce

1 litre (2 U.S. pints) milk or coconut milk

125 g (4 oz) butter or 120 ml (½ cup)
    olive oil
125 g (¾ cup) wholewheat flour
half a nutmeg, grated
5 egg yolks (save the whites!)
salt and pepper

Simmer the milk on low heat. Then, using a different pan from the milk, melt the butter or olive oil on low heat. Add the flour and nutmeg. Stir well with a whisk until a thick paste is formed. Gradually add the hot milk, whisking constantly, until the paste absorbs all the milk and becomes smooth. Add the egg yolks while stirring constantly. Add the salt and pepper. Stir.

The eggs

5 egg whites

Whip in a separate bowl, until they form soft peaks.

Putting the parts together

1. Mix the béchamel sauce, the millet and the vegetables.
2. Fold in the whipped egg whites, preserving as much air as possible.
3. Pour the soufflé into the greased baking dish and bake for 45 minutes until risen and golden.

Exotic carrot salad (V)

This is one of my favourite salads; it is always present on my table at festive meals.

Serves 4

2 very big carrots, grated on the roughest grater
1 orange, peeled and cut into cubes
40 g (¼ cup) raisins or dried cranberries

Toss together in a bowl.

Orange juice dressing

180 ml (¾ cup) orange juice
2 tbs honey
½ tbs coriander seeds, slightly toasted
    (this is a must!) and ground
1 tbs olive oil
a handful of fresh mint, finely chopped

Mix together.

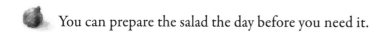 You can prepare the salad the day before you need it.

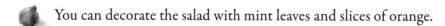 You can decorate the salad with mint leaves and slices of orange.

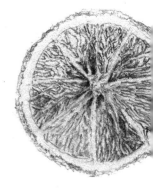

Choose-your-own fruit tarts

You will need a muffin tin with 12 holes. Preheat the oven to 150° C.

Makes 12 tarts

The pastry

150 g (5 oz) butter, softened
260 g (1 ¾ cups) wholewheat flour
60 ml (¼ cup) cold water
a pinch of salt

Work the butter into the flour with your fingertips, to the consistency of fine breadcrumbs. Add the water and go on mixing until you get an elastic dough. Flour a clean dry surface and roll out the dough to approximately 1 cm (½ in) thick. Using an upside-down cup or biscuit (cookie) cutter, cut 12 circles from it that are the right size to fit the holes in your muffin tin. Press each one into the muffin tin with your fingers, creating small tart cases. Pierce the cases with a fork and bake for 20–25 minutes.

The filling

½ quantity vanilla cream (see page 255)
600 g (about 1 lb) strawberries, raspberries, blueberries or cherries
180 ml (¾ cup) whipping cream, whipped with
1 ½ tbs sugar

Preparation of the tarts

When the tart cases are baked, cool them. Place 1 tbs vanilla cream in each one. On this place the fruit, either one kind or a mixture (you and each child can choose the fruit for their particular tart together), and top with the whipped cream.
　　Decorate each tart with a mint leaf and a piece of fruit.

RYE

Thursday is connected to Jupiter, the guardian of law, justice and maintaining public order. The name of this day in a number of European languages comes from the Latin 'Jovis'.

Rye grain is connected with Thursday. Rye loves light, air and cold. It has a strong root system and can grow well in acidic soil. It can survive storms, rain and snow, as well as rainless seasons. Of all the grains, rye seeds are the hardest to chew and to digest. Therefore rye helps to strengthen the digestive system and the building forces of the body. This grain is recommended for teenagers, who are in a stage of accelerated growth.

Rye is the grain of Northern Europe: of Russia and the Slavic countries.

Thursday menu

LEEK AND POTATO SOUP (V)

MULTICOLOUR STEW (V)

HENRIETTA'S RYE STEW (V)

LETTUCE AND TOFU SALAD (V)

YOGURT DELIGHTS

Leek and potato soup (V)

Serves 6–8

50 g (2 oz) butter or 60 ml (¼ cup) olive oil
1 tbs caraway seeds or ½ tbs caraway powder
2 medium leeks, chopped
2 large potatoes, peeled and cut into cubes
1 ½ litres (3 U.S. pints) vegetable stock or water
1 bunch of dill, chopped well
salt to taste
a bit of pepper

1. Melt the butter or heat the olive oil, add the caraway seeds and fry gently for 1 minute.
2. Add the leeks, potatoes and the stock or water, and cook until the potatoes are soft.
3. Add the salt and pepper.
4. Blend the soup with a hand blender until smooth. If the soup seems too thick, add more stock or water.
5. Add the dill, more salt and pepper if needed, and cover.
6. Serve with yogurt or sour cream.

If you like 'biting into' a soup, take some of it out before blending, then add it back before serving.

Washing leeks is a special job. I chop the bottom and a bit of the green end off, slice the leek lengthwise, hold it at the bottom with one hand and separate leaf after leaf with the other hand, washing out all the leftover mud.

I always feel sorry that people chop so much of the green end of the leek off. It can be chopped finely and included with the white rings.

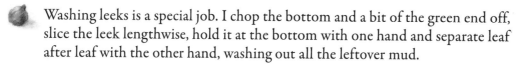

Multicolour stew (V)

When planning your cooking, take into account that about 2 hours will be needed for marinating the vegetables.

Serves 6–8

3 medium beetroots (beets), washed but not peeled, cut into cubes
2 carrots, cut lengthwise once and then crosswise into three
2 large onions, cut into quarters
1 celeriac, cut into large chunks

The marinade

½ tbs fresh ginger, grated
3 tbs apple juice concentrate (or pomegranate juice concentrate, if you can source it)
2 tbs lemon juice
5 tbs olive oil
600 ml (¼ cup) water

1. Put all the vegetables into an iron pot. (If you do not have one, you really should get one, or use a ceramic pot that can go into your oven.)
2. Mix the marinade and pour it onto the vegetables.
   Let it stand for two hours.
3. Bake for two hours with the lid on at 180° C (350° F).
   Or you can cook the stew on the stove: the result will be just as delicious. Check from time to time and add water if necessary.

Henrietta's rye stew (V)

Henrietta, a Dutch anthroposophical psychologist who was my guest, turned out to be an excellent cook. She taught me how to create this special dish.

Prepare the rye one day before.

Serves 6

200 g (1 cup) rye grain
480 ml (2 cups) water
and 60 ml ¼ cup water

Bring the rye to the boil in the water. Put a lid on the pot and turn off the heat. Cover the hot pot with a big towel and let it stand overnight. Add the extra water to the pot the next day and cook for 20 minutes or more on low heat, until the grains are soft.

olive oil for sautéing
2 medium onions, finely chopped

Sauté on low heat for 10 minutes, until golden.

1 celeriac, well washed and cut into cubes.
1 tbs honey
1 tbs fresh ginger, grated
5 dates, without the seeds, cut into cubes.

In a separate pot, cover the celeriac with water and cook for 10 minutes. Strain and add the honey, ginger and dates.

Mix all the ingredients together: the cooked rye, the fried onions and the celeriac and honey mixture.

You can prepare this dish without the honey and dates if you don't like sweet tastes.

You can also serve this with Mediterranean stew (see page 82).

Love what is good for you

The rye grain requires serious chewing. Even after lengthy cooking it is still quite hard. Lovers of healthy food will easily take to this dish; however I especially recommend it for those who are addicted to fast, pre-prepared meals. It will help to accustom their taste buds to healthy, nourishing food.

Every one of us needs healing, since we all hurt ourselves, each differently. For one person it may be a craving for sweets or pre-prepared foods, for another it may be cravings for alcohol or drugs, and others are addicted to hurting their bodies, to unhealthy relationships and more. There is no limit to the ways in which we injure ourselves. In the area of food I always knew what was good for me, but in other areas I have needed to work hard to choose what nourishes me. Everyone is in a different place with the processes of their inner work.

Once I wrote a note to myself and left it on the desk, so that I would see it many times a day: 'Love what is good for you. Do not desire what harms you.'

For me, this message was about the kind of men I chose – they were always the 'wrong' ones. But I believe that we only choose what we need in order to develop inwardly, and there had to be an end to these 'wrong' men, because I was utterly fed up with my love affairs. I came to understand that I was choosing men who would leave me or who I would leave, because in some way this was what I wanted. Then I had to find out why I was doing that.

It all came back to my father, who died when I was nine years old, and who I adored. You must understand that these revelations take a lifetime. Mine took 51 years. Usually these deep understandings are accompanied with great inner pain. Then a major letting-go must take place. If that happens you are free – clean of old patterns that hold you back – and in a way you are reborn. The pattern is hard to find. Mine was: man–love– abandonment. This was engraved in my soul at the age of nine. In order to find the man who would love me and who I could love, I had to separate from my father and stop holding onto my 'safe' pattern. In love you can look for many things (warmth, comfort, friendship), but not for security!

This statement, 'love what is good for you', can be applied to food as well. But hard as it is to wean ourselves from unhealthy relationships, it is just as hard to let go of food that is bad for us.

Lettuce and tofu salad (V)

Note that the tofu needs to marinate for 5 hours before preparing the rest of the salad.

Serves 6–8

300 g (10 oz) tofu, cut into cubes
60 ml (¼ cup) olive oil
1 tbs dried marjoram

} Marinate the tofu cubes for 5 hours.

half a lettuce, broken into small pieces by hand
1 sweet pepper (bell pepper), sliced into thin strips
1 cucumber, sliced
2 tomatoes, sliced
juice of a lemon

} Toss together with the soaked tofu and olive oil. Serve immediately.

Yogurt delights

Most of these recipes contain honey. Do you know that honey is medicine? Bees are connected to the sun not only in colour, but on a deep level. The queen bee – not in commercial honey production but in organic bee-keeping – flies up towards the sun with some male bees and is fertilised in the air, under the sunlight. The bee is the only creature in the world that does this! Bees extract nectar (the most heavenly part of the flower) and turn it into honey. Thus spirit is materialised. What we eat, when we eat honey, is really the light of the golden sun!

These yogurt shakes are tasty, sweet and refreshing! They can be turned into a dessert rather than a drink if you prefer.

All these drinks are to be mixed with a blender or shaker. Drink with a straw.

Date yogurt

240 ml (1 cup) yogurt (see page 62)
1 heaped tbs date paste, or 4 dates, seeded

Carob and honey yogurt

240 ml (1 cup) yogurt
1 tbs honey
1 tbs carob powder (often needs to be sifted since it can be chunky)

Cinnamon and honey yogurt

240 ml (1 cup) yogurt
1 tbs honey
1 tbs cinnamon powder

Fruit yogurt

The perfect alternative to commercially produced yogurt drinks!

240 ml (1 cup) yogurt
150 g (5 oz) mango, or another fruit (peach, apricot, melon, strawberry), peeled and
  with pits, stones or seeds removed

If the drink is not sweet enough, add honey.

Forest fruit yogurt

Serves 8–10

berry fruits mix (see page 187)   Chill the yogurt and fruit mix, then
500 ml (2 cups) yogurt   sprinkle fruit and granola on top.
a little granola for serving (see page 230)

OATS

Friday is connected to Venus (the Goddess and the planet), and the grain associated with the day is oats.

Oats are most familiar to us in their flattened form as rolled oats: the main ingredient of muesli, granola, hot porridge and many cookies. The oat groats in these recipes are whole, unflattened grains, more like barley: check for them in your local whole-food store.

Rolled oats are the only form of grain that it is possible to eat without cooking (in muesli). Oats completely absorb the forces of the sun and are therefore already 'cooked'.

Oats are richer in fats than other grains and therefore supply more heat in our digestive system. For this reason they are good to eat when we feel depressed, because in a depressed state the digestive system cools down or even 'freezes'.

Oats are high in protein, and are therefore also good food for animals.

Oats originated in cold northern Europe; oats are the basic food of the Celts and Scandinavians.

There is a school of thought that relates barley to Friday and oats to Tuesday. It's your choice! Be creative!!!

Friday menu (Sabbath meal)

ORANGE (PUMPKIN) SOUP (V)

OAT GROATS (SEE PAGE 68)

FRESH STIR-FRY WITH SOY AND HONEY SAUCE (V)

TOFU IN GADO-GADO (PEANUT) SAUCE (V)

SALAD (SEE PAGE 57)

**NUT TORTE WITH CHESTNUT CREAM
OR OMAMA'S CHOCOLATE CREAM**

HOT APPLE CIDER (NON-ALCOHOLIC) (V)

 This is a festive evening meal since in Israel Friday's sunset is the beginning
of the rest day, Shabbat. In Jewish and Israeli communities, families get together
and friends invite one another. It is a minor celebration that is very much present
in our life every week. It separates Friday from other days and, indeed, every
Friday evening is special.

Warm sweetness

Cooking pumpkin soup reminds me of a cold winter day from my childhood in Transylvania: the first of November, the day of the dead. On this day everyone goes to the cemetery to decorate the graves of their beloved ones with chrysanthemum flowers and candles. As darkness descends we all light the candles and transform the cemetery into a spectacle of lights. The air is filled with the smell of burning candles mingled with the scent of the flowers. People work quietly, encouraging us kids to whisper and keep calm instead of running around. Sadness for the loss of loved ones unites with an attentive activity for them.

I loved wandering on the paths of the cemetery and watching people's creativity, turning the graves into flowing forms of candles and flowers. As everyone was working, silently absorbed in memories, I could imagine the dead joining together in a circle dance, joyous at not being forgotten.

The end of this intimate ritual was the eating of pumpkin baked on an open fire and sold at the gate of the cemetery. How delicious it was! Rich in taste, steaming from the glowing coals, so comforting. Sitting next to mother on the bus that took us home, I put my head on her shoulder, closed my eyes and felt the grey salty tears shed for my dead transforming into an orange sweetness in my stomach.

Orange (pumpkin) soup (without orange) (V)

This 'orange' soup's flavour is perfect. The mixture of the saltiness and the sweetness of the vegetables has to reach such a level of harmony that when you eat this soup you feel like melting.

Amina, who was a cook in the restaurant, and I would make this soup together. Amina would make the 'physical body' of the soup: cleaning and cutting the vegetables, cooking and mashing them. Then she would call for me: 'Come, bring it to the heavens!'

I would add the spices, salt and sugar, then taste it. If the taste wasn't perfect I would say: 'Today it's a little cloudy, it's hard to reach the heavens.' And if the soup 'gave' itself to me easily, I would say: 'The sky is clear today!'

Serves 10–12

2 medium sweet potatoes, cubed
2 medium carrots, cubed
700 g (1 ½ lb) pumpkin, peeled and cubed
3 medium onions, diced
5 garlic cloves, whole
1 ½ litres (3 U.S. pints) vegetable stock or water

Put into a pot, bring to the boil, lower the heat and cook until the carrots are soft. Blend with a hand blender, then bring to the boil once more.

2–3 tbs brown sugar
salt and black pepper to taste
little red chilli, ground (optional)
¼ tsp nutmeg, grated
zest of half an orange
zest of half a lemon
half a bunch dill or marjoram, chopped

} Add.

60 ml (¼ cup) single or light cream, or
coconut milk (optional)

} To enrich the soup's taste, if you wish, add just before the end of the cooking time, then lower the heat so it doesn't boil.

croutons (see page 84) (optional)
dill, finely chopped, to decorate
saffron to decorate

This soup can be served with croutons.

When serving, sprinkle dill and saffron on top. The deep red colour of the saffron merges well with the light orange colour of the soup, and the green dill balances it all.

Fresh stir-fry with soy and honey sauce (V)

First you need to make a cup of soy and honey sauce to add to the stir-fry at the end.

Serves 8

6 tbs sesame oil
4 tbs sunflower oil
} Heat in a wok or frying pan or skillet.

4 carrots, cut into matchsticks
250 g cauliflower, broken into florets
} Add, and fry 3 minutes.

2 large onions, sliced
2 celery stalks, without the leaves, chopped
1 sweet pepper (bell pepper), cut into strips
250 g (9 oz) broccoli, broken into little florets
} Add and fry for another 3 minutes.

250 g (9 oz) white cabbage, finely cut
a handful of mushrooms, sliced
1 large courgette (zucchini), sliced
1 cup bean sprouts
} Add and fry for another 3 minutes.

1 cup soy and honey sauce (see below)
} Add and stir. Cover and keep cooking on a lower heat for 5 minutes, until the carrots and cauliflower become soft to your taste.

Sesame seeds, toasted
Spring onions (scallions), chopped
} Sprinkle on top to serve.

It is possible to add 300 g (10 oz) tofu, cut into cubes, to the second batch of vegetables. If using dried tofu, soak it in water and a bit of soy sauce for 2 hours before cooking.

117

Soy and honey sauce (V)

Have a jar of this sauce in the fridge all the time. It can keep refrigerated for months. It can be used for stir-fry, grains, almond burgers (see page 274), stuffed butternut squash (see page 183) and more.

Makes about 350 ml (1 ½ cups) of sauce

4 garlic cloves, crushed
1 tbs fresh ginger, grated or ½ tsp dry ginger
120 ml (½ cup) soy sauce
120 ml (½ cup) water
1 tbs apple vinegar
1 ½ tbs honey

Boil all the ingredients together.

½ tbs cornflour (cornstarch)
2 tbs water

Mix in a separate bowl, then add to the sauce to thicken it. Bring to the boil again and cook for 3 more minutes.

Tofu in gado-gado (peanut) sauce (V)

For the gado-gado sauce, you need soy and honey sauce (see above).

Start by soaking the tofu for 2 hours before cooking.

Serves 8–10

600 g (1 ¼ lb) tofu, cut into small cubes
60 ml (¼ cup) water
3 tbs soy sauce

> Soak for 2 hours.

sesame oil for frying
2 large onions, finely chopped

> Fry in a medium-sized pan until golden. Lower the heat.

½ cup peanut butter
1 cup soy and honey sauce (see above)

> Add and cook for 2 minutes until everything has mixed well together. Then add the tofu with the soaking liquid and cook for a further 10 minutes.

Spring onions (scallions), chopped

> Sprinkle on top to serve.

This dish is even better on the second day.

Nut torte with chestnut cream or Omama's chocolate cream

This torte is filled with either chestnut cream or Omama's chocolate cream, or both. The recipes for these are on the following pages.

You will need a round, 28 cm (11 in) diameter sprung cake tin, or a square pan, 36 x 36 cm (14 x 14 in).

Preheat the oven to 150° C (300° F).

6 egg whites
1 tbs brown sugar
— Whip together to form soft peaks.

6 egg yolks
5 tbs brown sugar
— Whip together in a separate bowl from the whites.

6 tbs walnuts or hazelnuts, finely ground
2 tbs wholewheat flour, or *matzah* flour
— Mix into the yolks.

Gently fold the yolk and nut mixture into the whipped egg whites.
Oil and line the cake tin, pour the mixture into it and bake for 20 minutes.

Putting the torte together

1 cup whipping cream, whipped with
2 tbs brown sugar

1. Cut the baked and cooled cake into 3 equal layers (if you have used a round tin), or into 3 equal strips (if you have used a large square tin).
2. Place one layer on a serving tray and pour half a quantity of chestnut cream (see page 122) onto it or half a quantity of chocolate cream (see page 123) (or, for real indulgence, both).
3. Place another layer of cake on top and pour the remaining chestnut cream or chocolate cream on it.
4. Place the last layer on top and cover the whole cake with the sweetened whipped cream, even the sides.
5. Sprinkle some toasted and ground nuts on the top and on the sides.

 You can also use more chestnut cream or chocolate cream for the top and sides instead of the whipped cream.

Chestnut cream

Making chestnut cream is a task for extremely bored or extremely hard-working people, because it takes a lot of time and patience!

It is possible to freeze the cream.
 You can buy chestnut cream in whole-food shops or you can replace it in this torte with Omama's chocolate cream (see page 123).

Makes about 750 g (1 ¹/₂ lb)

500 g (1 lb) chestnuts, in their shells
240 ml (1 cup) milk
100 g (½ cup) brown sugar
3 tbs rum

1. Cut a cross on each chestnut's shell.
2. Cover the chestnuts with water then add another 480 ml (2 cups). Put the lid on the pot and cook for an hour until the chestnuts are soft. Drain and cool.
3. Cut each chestnut in half and scoop out the inner part with a teaspoon. (This is the stage that takes patience.) Put this into a pot.
4. Add the sugar and milk. Cook for 10–15 minutes on a very low heat, until the chestnuts are soft.
5. Push the milky chestnuts through a sieve, or a mouli if you have one, to get a purée and to remove any stubbornly remaining shells.
6. Add the rum and stir.

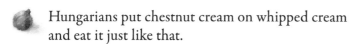

Hungarians put chestnut cream on whipped cream
and eat it just like that.

Omama's chocolate cream and chocolate sauce

150 g (¾ cup) brown sugar
180 ml (¾ cup) milk
3 tbs cocoa powder
200 g (7 oz) soft butter

1. Cook the sugar, cocoa and milk on a very low heat for about 20–30 minutes. Stir from time to time. The sauce should be thick-ish but not totally stiff. Take off the heat and cool.
2. Add the soft butter and mix well. You can use a whisk.

It is possible to add 60 g (½ cup) finely ground toasted walnuts (toasted in a toaster oven at 160° C (320° F) for 5–10 minutes). The result is delicious!

Chocolate sauce

In order to get a chocolate sauce for pouring on ice cream or pancakes, replace the milk with water and add the butter to the hot sauce immediately after it has thickened.

Hot apple cider (non-alcoholic) (V)

Makes 2 litres (4 U.S. pints)

1 ¾ litres (3 ½ U.S. pints) water
4 cinnamon sticks
4 cloves
1 apple, cut into cubes
1 orange, sliced (optional)
330 ml (11 U.S. fl oz) apple juice concentrate
lemongrass, geranium, mint or lemon balm

1. Boil the water with the cinnamon and cloves for 15 minutes.
2. Add the apple cubes and orange slices and cook for another 2 minutes.
3. Take off the heat, add the apple juice concentrate and one of the tea plants. Cover the pot.

CORN

Saturday, Saturn ♄ Saturnus, dies Saturni, Shabbat

Saturday is the day of Saturn. In Hebrew tradition, this is the day on which God rested from the labour of creation.

The grain connected to Saturday is corn. Of all the grains, corn has the strongest connection to the earth. It is rich in starch and is therefore easily digested and is a good source of instant energy. Many products are made from corn – in the food industry and in other industries – including ethanol, which is often added to motor fuel.

Corn is related to the melancholic temperament, which carries the burden of earthly life. It is passive in its activities but active within, taken up with contemplation and reflection.

The origin of corn is in the West – in the Americas.

Saturday Menu

COURGETTE (ZUCCHINI) AND RED PEPPER (BELL PEPPER) IN GINGER SAUCE (V)

BAKED CORIANDER (CILANTRO) POLENTA

APPLE AND WALNUT SALAD (V)

FRUIT IN CRISPY BEER BATTER

Courgette (zucchini) and red pepper (bell pepper) in ginger sauce (V)

This is suitable as a side dish to accompany any grain.

Serves 8–12

  sesame oil for frying
  2 sweet red peppers (bell peppers), cut into thin strips
  6 medium courgettes (zucchinis), cut into thick strips
  5 garlic cloves, chopped roughly
  4 tbs soy sauce
  1 tbs fresh ginger, grated
  85 g (½ cup) blanched almonds, toasted

1. Heat the oil in a pan and cook the peppers (bell peppers) for 5–10 minutes on medium heat, until soft.
2. Add the courgettes (zucchini) and all the other ingredients, apart from the almonds. Cover and keep cooking for 5 minutes. No need to add water. Don't overcook; let the peppers remain crispy.
3. When serving, sprinkle the almonds on top.

Toasted almonds

Toast almonds by dry frying them in a pan on low heat for 10 minutes, stirring continuously.

Baked coriander (cilantro) polenta

Serves 8–12

You will need a square baking pan, 32 x 24 cm (12.5 x 9.5 in).

Preheat oven to 180° C (350° F).

This delicious dish has two parts to prepare:

> Frying the vegetables
> Cooking the polenta

Vegetables

olive oil for sautéing
5 medium onions, finely chopped

} In a separate pan, sauté for 15 minutes until golden

1 tbs brown sugar
1 carrot, grated
1 sweet pepper (bell pepper), cut into strips
1 courgette (zucchini), sliced

} Add to the onion and sauté for a further 10 minutes.

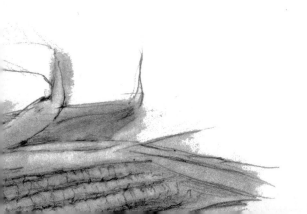

Polenta

1 litre (4 cups) milk   Boil in a pot.
240 ml (1 cup) water

½ cup polenta (cornmeal)   Add and cook on low heat for 3–5 minutes while stirring constantly. Turn off the heat.

150 g (6 oz) butter or 180 ml (¾ cup) olive oil
1 bunch fresh coriander (cilantro), chopped (if you are a coriander-hater, use dill)
½ tsp coriander seeds, lightly oven-toasted
salt and pepper

Add to the mixture and stir well.

Add the fried vegetables to the polenta and stir. Pour this mixture into the greased baking pan. Make sure that the top of the mixture is even.

Bake for 45 minutes.

- You can choose to add 65 g (½ cup) grated cheese (parmesan, cheddar or any other you fancy) into the polenta mixture.

- Instead of using carrots, sweet pepper (bell pepper) or courgette (zucchini), you can use cooked peas or any other vegetables you like.

- You can place round slices of tomatoes on the top of the mixture to make the bake look attractive.

Apple and walnut salad (V)

Serves 4–6

8 lettuce leaves, chopped
2 large cucumbers, chopped
60 g (½ cup) bean sprouts (see page 64)
1 apple, diced
25 g (¼ cup) dry cranberries
3 spring onions (scallions), chopped
30 g (¼ cup) walnuts, toasted and chopped
5 tbs olive oil
juice of half a lemon

Toss all the ingredients together.

Fruit in crispy beer batter

Makes 20–30 fruit pieces

Serves 10

The batter

150 g (1 cup) wholewheat flour
1 egg
a pinch of salt
2 tbs sugar
3 tbs oil
240 ml (1 cup) beer

Mix all the ingredients.

The fruit

banana, cut into 4–5 cm chunks
apple (without seeds) or pear, ½ cm-thick slices
dates, seeded
pineapple pieces
lychees

sunflower oil for deep frying

Dip each piece of fruit into the batter and then carefully drop them into the preheated oil. Fry for 5–8 minutes until golden brown. Place them on a paper towel so some of the oil drains off. Serve immediately.

Serve with home-made ice cream (see page 93) or honey-butter sauce (see page 229) or, for corrupted indulgence, both.

The listed fruits are only suggestions. You can go wild with others.

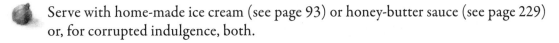

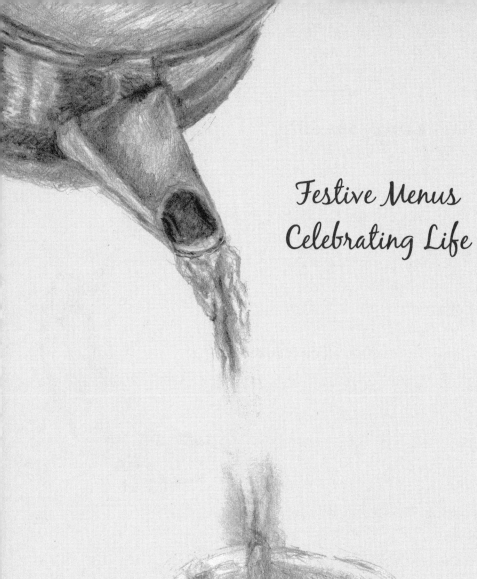

Festive Menus
Celebrating Life

Meals with friends

As a young girl, I had a wild soul. I was a real tomboy who did things that only boys would do. I climbed trees, and when we played hide-and-seek I always loved to hide in dangerous, exciting places so that usually no one could find me. I always wore trousers and did not enjoy dressing up. I never wore jewellery and preferred to play with boys.

As a teenager I socialised more with groups of boys, being part of gangs (we were by no means dangerous to the public, but more like the trio gang from my favourite book, *To Kill a Mockingbird*). Girls' conversation really bored me (except for one best girl friend, with whom I had endless conversations about love).

Today I have many interesting women as well as some men friends. Axel Ewald is one of them. We share two great loves: swimming and cooking. In the summer time we swim every morning in Harduf's pool in parallel lanes. Other swimmers at Harduf know that those are 'our' lanes and leave them vacant for us.

We love to surprise each other with unique dishes. When I invite Axel and his wife to a meal, I want to amaze them with my culinary creativity. I invest not only in the cooking, but also in the planning of the meal, which is always exciting. Axel's meals are always a creation of their own as well.

We usually eat together on Fridays, with the table beautifully arranged and the candles lit. We sing Shabbat songs and drink good wine – without which there is no perfect meal for us (although I know that it causes regression in my spiritual development...).

Jutka invites Axel

FATMA'S AUBERGINE (EGGPLANT) SALAD (V)

PARSLEY AND FRESH CORIANDER (CILANTRO) PESTO (V)

FATMA'S TAHINI (V)

KEREN'S ROLLS

CELERY SOUP (V)

**PEPPERS (BELL PEPPERS) STUFFED
WITH FETA AND RICOTTA**

SIMPLE GREEN SALAD (V)

MOTHER'S CHERRY CAKE

But it's so delicious...

Fatma Khaabia was already working at Harduf's restaurant when I arrived. She was washing dishes and working as a kitchen hand. She was quite impossible to handle, totally incapable of functioning in a team. After a few months Amina (like Fatma, a Bedouin girl working with us) and I agreed on firing her, but as time passed I could not do it. I guess my education from communist Romania, where workers were always considered 'holy' and definitely above the exploiting capitalist boss (which in this case was me), had had a stronger influence on me than I had imagined.

So there we were, stuck with Fatma. I started thinking about her a lot after working hours, and slowly the picture of a very frustrated Fatma appeared in front of me. Then the great idea of giving Fatma a cooking task arose. I taught her to make our vegetable pie. To my great surprise, her pie was not only perfect but, for the first time, I saw a smiling Fatma. Then I understood the healing power of creating food. Slowly, slowly, I taught Fatma all my dishes. She became a happy cook and I, having become unnecessary in the kitchen, an unhappy manager, being responsible for the dry administrative side of the restaurant. I always envy the cooking girls in the juicy kitchen.

Today Fatma manages the kitchen with a firm hand. She is the queen there. She has her own Bedouin world-view that took me a long time to understand.

During my sixteen years of 'marriage' with Fatma, I have learned when I should stand my ground and when it is better to yield. With her deep wisdom and my ability to analyse situations, we succeeded in rising above our conflicts to a place of quiet clarity. Of course even there, it is stormy sometimes.

Fatma has internalised the idea that roots nourish the head and therefore also human thought. She understands that it is advisable to eat leaves to create a balanced soul, and flowers to strengthen the will forces.

One day she hung twelve rainbow-coloured silk balls in the kitchen and declared that they were the twelve archangels.

When I said that they were not suitable for the kitchen, she insisted that they would bring luck. I gave in, understanding that anthroposophy has penetrated Fatma, and hoping she is right about our luck.

But when it comes to her aubergine (eggplant) salad and I try to explain that frying ruins the vegetables, she just looks at me with a wide smile and says: 'but it's so delicious'.

The angels stayed in the kitchen, the customers have been enjoying the aubergine salad and I have learned how to live in a healthy, working relationship...

Fatma's aubergine (eggplant) salad (V)

Serves 5–6

plenty of sunflower oil for frying
1 kg (2 lb) aubergine (eggplant), peeled and cut
    into cubes, size 1–1 ½ cm (½ in)

Deep-fry on medium heat until golden. Place on paper towels for a few minutes, move to a bowl.

half a bunch parsley, well chopped
4 cloves garlic, crushed
½ tsp salt
½ tsp cumin powder
3 tbs tomato paste

Add all the ingredients to the aubergine bowl and mix.

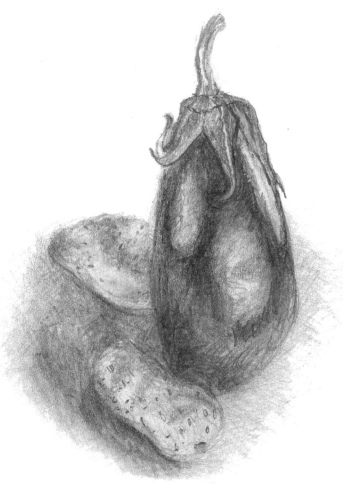

Parsley and fresh coriander (cilantro) pesto (v)

This spread is great for sandwiches, or with omelette, Bulgarian cheese, feta cheese, tofu, aubergine salad, tahini and more. It keeps for 10 days refrigerated.

2 bunches of parsley, without stalks
1 bunch of fresh coriander (cilantro), without stalks
1 garlic clove (or more, by taste)
60 g (½ cup) walnuts
180 ml (¾ cup) olive oil

Blend all the ingredients in a food processor and place in a jar.
Keep refrigerated.

Fatma's tahini (V)

Makes 600 ml (2 ½ cups)

100 g (1 cup) tahini
240 ml (1 cup) water
1 tsp salt
80 ml (⅓ cup) lemon juice
1 small bunch parsley, finely chopped
3 garlic cloves, crushed
¼ tsp cumin, ground
pinch black pepper

Mix all the ingredients in a food processor, or in a bowl with a whisk. Keep refrigerated.

Keren's rolls

Keren, who works with us at Harduf restaurant, taught me how to make these rolls. Although I usually prefer yeast-free sourdough rye bread and do not think that yeast is very healthy, it is hard for me to resist Keren's rolls filling the space with the great smell of freshly baked bread...

Makes 20–25 rolls

Preheat oven to 220° C (420° F).

¾ tbs dry yeast or 30 g (1 oz) fresh yeast
1 tbs brown sugar
120 ml (½ cup) warm milk
3 tbs wholewheat flour

} Mix together, then leave in a warm place to ferment until the mix doubles in size.

530 g (3 ½) cups wholewheat flour
1 tsp salt
3 tbs seeds (flax, sesame, sunflower), with extra for decoration
80 g (3 oz) butter, melted, or 80 ml (⅓ cup) olive oil
240 ml (1 cup) warm milk
2 eggs, beaten, plus extra for glazing

1. Mix the flour, salt and seeds.
2. Add the butter or oil, milk, eggs and mix.
3. Add the yeast mixture, stir and knead well. Place the dough in a warm place to rise until it doubles in size.
4. Separate the dough into 20–25 pieces and roll them into balls (or knead into long sausages to make a bagel shape).
5. Place the rolls onto an oiled tray. Brush them with beaten egg. Sprinkle sesame, flax or sunflower seeds on top, leave for 20 more minutes to rise then bake for 15 minutes.

Celery soup (V)

olive oil or butter for frying
3 medium onions, chopped
1 medium leek, chopped

} Fry until golden.

1 bunch of celery with leaves, chopped
3 medium potatoes, cut into small cubes.
2 litres (4 U.S. pints) soup stock or water
1 tsp whole caraway or ½ tsp ground caraway
1 tsp salt
black pepper

} Add to the onions and cook until the potatoes are very soft. Blend the soup. Adjust the salt and pepper to taste.

light or single cream or coconut milk (optional)
saffron or dill or parsley to decorate the soup
croutons (see page 84)

You can add light cream or coconut milk. Before serving, sprinkle saffron (only for decoration, so if you don't have it use a dill or parsley leaf) on top of the soup. Serve with croutons.

 Organic celery bunches are often smaller than non-organic.
If you are using non-organic celery, use a little less than specified above.

Peppers (bell peppers) stuffed with feta and ricotta

A perfect dish for a hot summer's day, perhaps accompanied by cooked quinoa, steamed broccoli, exotic carrot salad and a salad of green leaves.

Serves 12 (6 if they are very hungry!)

Preheat oven to 150° C (300° F).

olive oil for frying
2 medium onions, chopped, or 2 leeks, finely sliced
100 g (3 oz) mushrooms, sliced
2 small carrots, grated
1 large courgette (zucchini), grated
3 cloves of garlic, crushed

Fry the onions or leeks for 5 minutes. Add the other ingredients and keep frying for 5 more minutes.

200 g (7 oz) feta cheese, grated
300 g (10 ½ oz) ricotta (see page 62) or our labane (see page 63), or both
2 eggs, beaten
half a bunch of dill, finely chopped

Mix in a bowl. Add the fried vegetables to the mixed cheeses and eggs.

6 red or yellow peppers (bell peppers)

1. Cut the peppers in half lengthwise and take the seeds out. Fill the two halves with the cheesy vegetable mix and place on an oiled baking pan or tray.
2. Bake for 20–25 minutes, until the filling turns golden.

You can sprinkle grated parmesan over the peppers a few minutes before turning the oven off.

We pour a bit of single cream on the peppers when we heat them for a customer. This makes them juicy rather than dry.

For decoration you can put dill or parsley on the peppers. Its greenness with the redness of the peppers and the whiteness of the cheese looks very appetising.

Simple green salad (V)

I have not indicated quantities for this salad. They are up to you!

Black radishes are very bitter and spicy (sharp) but help prevent catching a cold. In the house for people with special needs where I worked in England, they used them as medicine: one teaspoon of finely grated black radish, honey and lemon juice three times a day.

lettuce leaves, all kinds of colours, ripped into large chunks
mixed leaves – rocket (arugula), mustard leaves and more
spring onion (scallions), chopped   } Place in a bowl.
black radish, grated (small amount)
sunflower seeds toasted with soy sauce (see page 85)

Simple dressing

olive oil
a little Dijon mustard   } Mix and pour over salad leaves.
juice of a lemon
a little honey

Cherry cake

It was early morning on a cool summer day. The rhythmical sound of light rain was mixed with the noise of some activity. I slept next door to the kitchen in the living room, so when Mother started pottering, I usually woke up too.

On that day though, in my holiday spirit, I lazed in bed for quite a while, in the blurred state between dreamland and reality. I heard the singing of Mother's favourite blackbird, the barking of Janos' dogs, the *kotkodacsolas* (scrabbling) of our hens and the sharp violent *kukkorekolas* (cock-a-doodle-doo) of Pityu, our colourful rooster. Finally, Mother's pottering got me out of bed, curiosity winning over laziness.

The gas oven was spreading a delicious warmth on that rainy morning. Mother was standing at our old wooden table, which had witnessed the stories of many generations. She was mixing white flour with butter, eggs and a fluffy yeast mixture. Next to her stood a big bowl of cherries.

'Could you pit these cherries for me?' she asked, and I felt honoured. It was quite rare that Mother asked for help. I pitted the deep red, fat cherries. It was a messy job, with their juice splashing all over me, but a pleasurable one, since some of them found their way into my mouth. Nowhere else in the world have I eaten cherries with the same sweet taste.

'Now squeeze the juice out of them by hand, add cinnamon and sugar to them and pour them on the raised dough waiting in the baking tin. Once you have done that I can put the other half of the dough on the cherries and bake the cake,' Mother instructed me.

'Next time I come I will write this recipe down,' I said, feeling too cosy to get up and get my notebook. Mother did not look up, but said,

'Write it down now!'

'What are you talking about, Anyu?' I asked, grasping the message about the approaching end. 'You are so strong, working all day in the garden and with your chickens.'

'Get a pen and write the recipe.' An unusual firmness in her voice made me get up and fetch my notebook.

Six years have passed by since Mother left us. I still come home every summer. Our summer house is locked up for the whole year until I come. Weeds have overgrown the garden, the vegetables have disappeared and only the roses survive. Most of the fruit trees have dried out and those left are not pruned and have very few fruit. The last of the chickens that Mother hatched are gone. Only Janos is still there.

He brings me a basket full of cherries from his garden. I make the cherry cake. My brother, sisters and all our children come in the afternoon. A few days ago we celebrated my niece's wedding and for this rare occasion we all came from the three corners of the world. We have not been together like this since Mother's funeral.

I take the cake out of the oven, put icing sugar laced with cinnamon on it, and cut it. Everyone is eating a piece of the steaming, juicy cake. They say it is as delicious as Mother's. I look at them and say nothing.

Mother's cherry cake

You will need a square tin, 36 x 36 cm (14 x 14 in).
Preheat oven to 150° C (300° F).

The dough

20 g (¾ oz) fresh yeast or 1 tbs dry yeast
120 ml (½ cup) warm milk
3 tbs brown sugar
1 tbs wholewheat flour

> Mix in a bowl. Put in a warm place for 15 minutes until the mixture ferments and rises.

530 g (3 ½ cups) wholewheat flour, sifted
a pinch of salt
200 g (7 oz) very soft butter
2 egg yolks
2 tbs sour cream

> Pile the sifted flour on a large surface (your table for example) and create a volcano shape, with a hole in the middle. Pour the yeast mixture into the hole, add the butter, yolks and sour cream. Gently start working the added ingredients into the flour until they become one unit. Knead until the dough becomes soft but not sticky. (If it is sticky, add flour.) Divide into two halves.

A suggestion for the tired, has-no-time or lazy baker: you can mix the dough in an electric mixer. Mix on low speed for 5 minutes. Continue on higher speed until the dough looks united and soft but not sticky. It might need more flour if too sticky.

The filling

1 kg (2 lb) cherries, pitted and the juice squeezed out
    by hand (with an apron on!)
100 g (½ cup) brown sugar
60 g (½ cup) walnuts or pecans, finely chopped
zest of a lemon, grated
½ tsp cinnamon

    Mix in a bowl.

2 tbs semolina or breadcrumbs

1. Roll half of the dough with a rolling pin on a floured surface. Aim to make it the shape of your cake tin and about 1 ½ cm (½ in) thick. Grease the tin with oil or butter and place this flattened dough on its bottom.
2. Spread the semolina or breadcrumbs on the dough (they will 'drink up' the leftover juice of the cherries).
3. Then pour the cherry mixture onto the dough.
4. Roll out the other half of the dough, similar to the first half. Place it over the cherries.
5. Brush with a beaten egg. With a fork, make holes all over the dough.
6. Bake for 45–50 min.
7. Cool before slicing. You can sprinkle icing sugar (powdered sugar) on top (sometimes laced with cinnamon...).

Instead of cherries, you can use coarsely grated apples.

Axel invites Jutka

OLIVE SPREAD (V)

LABANE AND AVOCADO SPREAD

SHMULIKIM (BAKED OLIVE BITES)

SUMMER VEGETABLE SOUP WITH NOODLES (V)

LEEK, POTATO AND COURGETTE (ZUCCHINI) BAKE

BUCKWHEAT OR QUINOA OR MILLET BURGERS

AXEL'S BEETROOT (BEET), FENNEL AND ORANGE SALAD (V)

AXEL'S LEMONGRASS AND FRUIT DRINK (V)

CHOCOLATE MOUSSE COCONUT MERINGUE

Olive spread (V)

This spread is salty but very delicious. It is perfect on sandwiches with cheeses, omelettes or fried tofu slices.

Makes 500 g (1 lb)

250 g (9 oz) green olives, pitted
4 cloves of garlic
120 ml (½ cup) olive oil
100 g (3 oz) pine nuts or walnuts
100 g (3 oz) dried tomatoes
A handful of fresh basil (optional)

Mix together in the food processor.

Labane and avocado spread

Serves 4

1 large ripe avocado
2 tbs labane (see page 63) or cream cheese
3 tbs olive oil
2 cloves of garlic, crushed
2 tbs lemon juice
salt

1. Mash the avocado with a fork.
2. Add all the other ingredients and mix.
3. Serve with rye bread or rice cakes.

Shmulikim (baked olive bites)

Serves 10–15

Preheat the oven to 180° C (350° F).

100 g (3 oz) butter
225 g (1 ½ cups) wholewheat flour
1 tsp baking powder
salt to taste
125 g (4 ½ oz) labane (see page 63) or cream cheese
100 g (3 oz) feta cheese, grated
olives, pitted

1. Mix all the ingredients, except the olives, either by hand or in a mixer. Place the dough in the refrigerator for an hour.
2. Separate the dough into small balls, flatten, place an olive in the centre of each ball, close tight.
3. Place the stuffed balls onto an oiled tray and bake for 10–15 minutes, until golden.

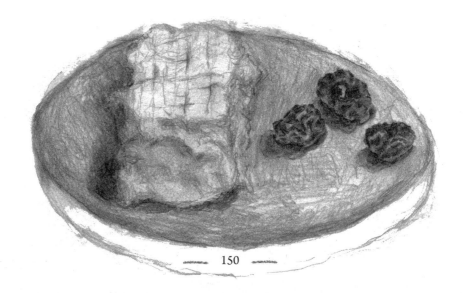

Summer vegetable soup with noodles (V)

Serves 10–12

2 large leeks, finely sliced
150 g (5 oz) sweetcorn or peas
half a celeriac, grated
2 celery stalks with leaves, finely chopped
2 ½ litres (5 U.S. pints) vegetable stock or water
half a bunch coriander (cilantro), whole

Cover the vegetables with the stock or water and cook for 25 minutes, until soft.

1 tsp fresh ginger, grated
2 tbs vinegar or lemon juice
black pepper
1 tsp salt
60 ml or 4 tbs soy sauce
1 can (400 ml, 14 U.S. fl oz) coconut milk
50 g (1 ½ oz) rice noodles

Add and cook another 10 minutes, until the noodles are soft.

1 courgette (zucchini), finely sliced

Add after you have taken the soup off the heat.

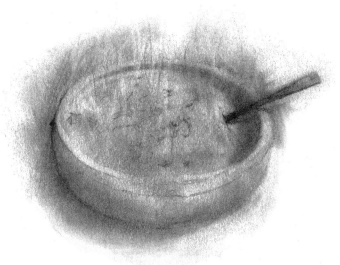

Leek, potato and courgette (zucchini) bake

Serves 4–6

You will need a deep baking dish, 23 x 35 cm (9 x 14 in).
Preheat oven to 150° C (300° F).

2 large potatoes
olive oil or butter for frying
2 medium leeks (or 1 large one)
2 medium courgettes (zucchinis)
480 ml (2 cups) sour cream or coconut milk
1 egg, beaten
salt to taste
black pepper

1. Cover the potatoes in water and cook for 20 minutes, until they are soft (so a knife can easily go through).
2. Cool, peel (only if not organic) and cut into large slices. Oil the baking dish and place the slices in it.
3. Wash the leeks well and cut into large slices. Heat the olive oil or butter and fry for 10 minutes until golden.
4. Cut the courgettes (zucchinis) into large strips and add to the leeks. Keep cooking for 5 minutes.
5. Place the leeks and courgettes (zucchini) on the potatoes in the baking dish.
6. Mix the cream or coconut milk, egg, salt and pepper and pour the mix over the vegetables.
7. Bake for 30–40 minutes, until golden.

This dish doesn't 'behave well' the next day, so finish eating it the day you bake it.

Buckwheat or quinoa or millet burgers

Makes 16 burgers

200 g (1 cup) buckwheat, quinoa or millet (or a mixture of two of these)

Cook the chosen grain or grains according to the table on page 68–69.
Move to a bowl.

olive oil for frying
1 large onion, chopped } Fry. Add to the bowl.

4 cloves of garlic, crushed
2 carrots, grated
1 celery stalk with leaves, finely chopped
½ tsp salt
half a bunch parsley
½ tsp sweet paprika
black pepper
2 eggs, beaten
2 tbs rye flour or wholewheat flour
sunflower oil for frying } Add to the bowl and mix.

Separate into balls, flatten to form burger shapes, then fry in sunflower oil on a
medium heat. Alternatively, you can oven-bake them for 15 minutes at 150° C
(300° F).
Serve with sweet and sour sauce (see page 275).

Axel's beetroot (beet), fennel and orange salad (v)

Serves 4–6

Consider making this a day in advance to allow the flavours to mingle.

2 large beetroots (beets)
half a bulb fennel, finely sliced
1 orange, peeled and cut into cubes

Seed dressing

1 tsp coriander seeds
6 tbs olive oil
2 tbs balsamic vinegar
½ tbs dark mustard seeds

1. Cook the beetroots (beets) in boiling water for 20 minutes, until a knife pierces them easily. Peel and cut into cubes (once cooked they are easily peeled by hand).
2. Place the beetroots (beets), fennel and orange cubes in a bowl.
3. Toast the coriander seeds in a frying pan or skillet for 5 minutes on medium heat, while stirring. Or bake them in the oven at 150° C (300° F) for 10 minutes. Be careful not to burn them.
4. Mix the dressing ingredients, pour onto the vegetables. Leave to marinate for a few hours or a day before serving.

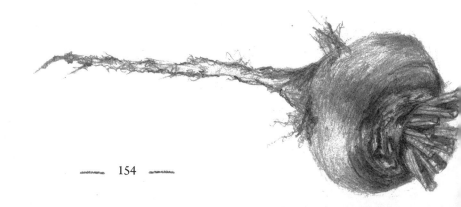

Axel's lemongrass and fruit drink (V)

Makes 2 litres (4 U.S. pints)

2 litres (4 U.S. pints) water
a handful of lemongrass leaves
330 ml (11 U.S. fl oz) bottle of concentrated apple or pear juice
lemon slices
fresh mint, or geranium

1. Pour boiling water over the lemongrass. Let it stand for 10 minutes. Chill.
2. After the lemongrass tea has cooled, add the concentrated juice, lemon and mint or geranium, for a zesty summer drink.

Be careful not to add too many leaves. Herb teas are like homeopathic medicine and they are best when gentle in taste.

Chocolate mousse coconut meringue

You will need a 28 cm diameter pie dish.
Preheat oven to 180° C (350° F).

Meringue base (baked)

6 egg whites (keep the yolks!)
150 g (¾ cup) brown sugar
100 g (1 ½ cups) desiccated coconut

1. Whip the egg whites and sugar until firm.
2. Add the coconut and gently fold it into the egg whites.
3. Oil the pie dish, pour the mixture into it and bake for 15 minutes. Take out of the oven and cool.
4. While the base is baking, make the filling.

Mousse filling (not baked)

200 g (7 oz) dark chocolate
1 tsp ground ginger or ½ tsp fresh ginger, grated
6 egg yolks
480 ml (2 cups) whipping cream
6 tbs brown sugar
preserved ginger and pine nuts for decoration (optional)

1. Melt the chocolate using a double pan (a pan or bowl resting in another pan of boiling water).
2. Add the ginger to the chocolate.
3. Add the yolks and stir.
4. Whip the cream and sugar and add to the chocolate mixture.
5. Pour the filling onto the baked coconut base (after it cools). Keep refrigerated.
6. If you want, decorate with preserved ginger strips and pine nuts.

Homesickness

After Father's early death – he was 51 years old – his brother Imre became our guardian. He helped my mother financially and regularly visited us. I got very attached to him. So when, two years later, he told us that his immigration request had been accepted and he was leaving for America, I was very sad. To ease my pain he suggested that I accompany him to Bucharest to see him off on the plane. This was a great excitement for me at the age of eleven; we were going to fly to our capital city, where I had never been before.

We spent two days in Bucharest. Imre showed me the city. He took me to a big park – Cismigiu Gardens – where swans swam on the lake and we went rowing in a small boat. Then the day of his departure came and his friends took us to Otopeni International Airport. After a heartbreaking goodbye, Imre disappeared and I stayed with his friends next to a huge window from which we could see people boarding their planes. Imre got onto a very big Boeing jet. As it took off, its silver body shining in the morning sun, I thought, 'One day I also want to fly to freedom.'

After high school and a very successful matriculation exam, no one understood why I did not apply to university. Only I knew that it was because I wanted to leave Romania. A Jewish classmate of mine told me about all the steps he took to emigrate to Israel. It took me a year to get the rare, precious object that many in Romania dreamt about – a passport with a visa in it for Israel.

My mother accompanied me to Bucharest. She stood at the huge window of Otopeni airport and watched her beloved 20-year-old daughter board the silver monster. As I walked up the steps from the tarmac into the jet I wanted to look back and wave to her. I felt her tears mingling with mine. But I had to move on; I wanted to be free! At that moment I decided to always look forward. With an aching heart I entered the plane. As it took off, an exhilarating joy of freedom spread over me. My Uncle Imre had come over from America and was waiting for me at Ben Gurion Airport in Tel Aviv.

Never in my life have I regretted my decision to leave Romania. The freedom that I thought was waiting for me in Tel Aviv became a much longer journey than an airplane could make.

Yet homesickness remains with me; it became an inseparable partner. To ease my yearning, I return to Várad (Oradea) twice a year. I roam the streets of my youth, I watch the river Körös carrying many secrets, and I shop at a small but busy 'peasant' market for vegetables, fruit and cheese. But most of my time I spend in the Hegy, our summer house. Every morning I drink coffee with Janos, who is still energetic in spite of his old age. My sister, Mazsola, my only sibling left in Varad after our brother's death, comes and stays with me. We cook, read, talk, quarrel and play cards. Total rest!

The phone rings. Mazsola picks up the phone and passes it to me. It is Fatma. She tells me that everything is going well in the restaurant in Harduf. Adam, my only son, comes to eat every day and helps when it is busy. Keren, who joined our team recently, made an Eszterházy torte and the customers loved it. It is very hot and Keren waters our small vegetable garden every day. The cherry tomatoes, lettuce, celery, Swiss chard, basil, thyme and rosemary are all growing and there are lots of baby lemons on our trees.

'The grapes at your house are ripening well too,' Fatma says. Three years ago Janos cut twenty grape sticks off our grape vines in the Hegy, and I planted them in the garden of my new home in Harduf. Now they are bearing their first fruit.

Then Fatma passes the phone to Fahed, my man, who I found after fifty years of loneliness. We talk for a few moments. As I put the phone down I feel homesick. I want to taste my own grapes – and Keren's Eszterházy torte.

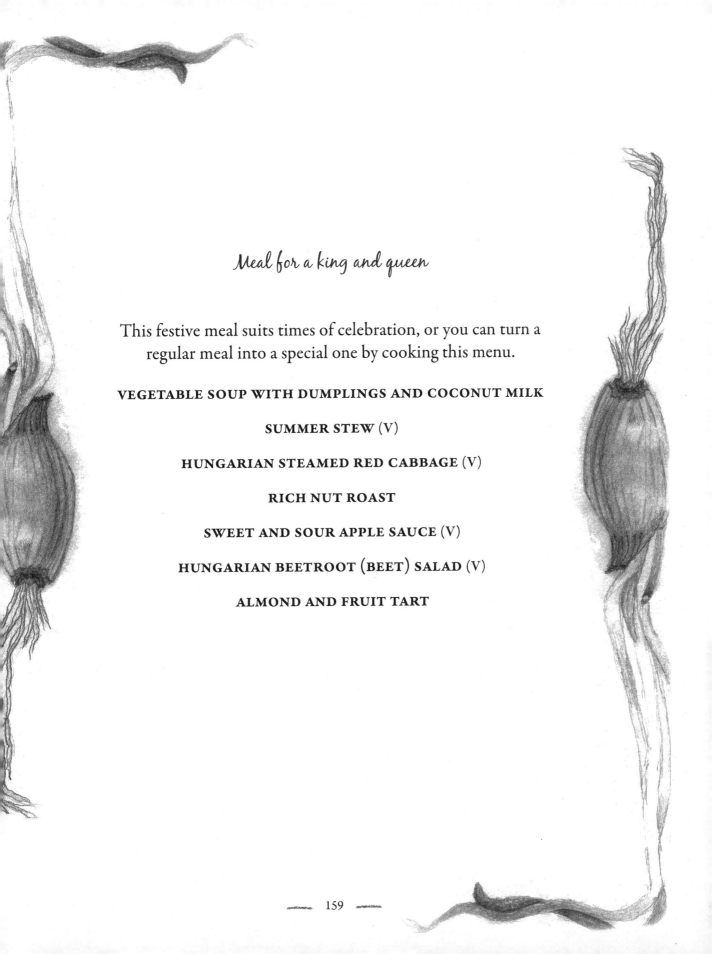

Meal for a king and queen

This festive meal suits times of celebration, or you can turn a regular meal into a special one by cooking this menu.

VEGETABLE SOUP WITH DUMPLINGS AND COCONUT MILK

SUMMER STEW (V)

HUNGARIAN STEAMED RED CABBAGE (V)

RICH NUT ROAST

SWEET AND SOUR APPLE SAUCE (V)

HUNGARIAN BEETROOT (BEET) SALAD (V)

ALMOND AND FRUIT TART

Vegetable soup with dumplings and coconut milk

Serves 10–12

olive oil for sautéing
3 medium onions or 1 large leek, chopped
quarter of a cauliflower, broken into florets
1 sweet potato, cut into cubes
3 carrots, finely sliced
2 kohlrabi, cut into strips, or 5 cabbage leaves, cut into strips
2 litres (4 U.S. pints) soup stock or water
salt
black pepper
1 bunch fresh coriander (cilantro) or dill, finely chopped
2 large courgettes (zucchinis), finely sliced
1 400 ml (14 U.S.fl oz) can coconut milk – look for one without chemicals
(this is hard to find but it does exist)
5 tbs soy sauce (optional)

1. Sauté all the vegetables, apart from the courgette (zucchini),
   in plenty of olive oil in a large pot.
2. Cover the vegetables in stock or water. Simmer until the sweet potato
   becomes soft.
3. Add the dumplings (see below) and keep cooking for another 5 minutes.
4. Turn off the flame. Add courgette (zucchini), coriander (cilantro) or dill,
   salt, pepper, coconut milk and soy sauce.

 Alternatively, you can decide not to fry the vegetables,
and simply cook them in the stock or water.

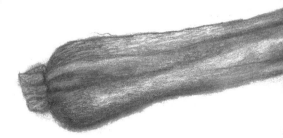

Dumplings

Hungarians love dumplings, not only in soups but also as a main dish!

1 egg, beaten
75 g (½ cup) white or wholewheat flour
2–4 tbs water
¼ tsp salt

1. Combine all the ingredients, then beat gently with a spoon until smooth.
2. Leave for 10 minutes.
3. Place a piece of the soft dough about 2 cm (just under 1 in) across on the tip of a spoon, then put the spoon into the hot soup. Repeat until all your dumpling mix is gone.

To make dumplings as a main dish, boil water and spoon the dough into it. Cook for 5–10 minutes, drain the dumplings, put a bit of oil on them, and serve with sour cream and chopped fresh dill. To westerners it sounds strange, but this is really yummy!

Kneidlach (matzah flour dumplings)

You can't imagine how many varieties of *kneidlach* exist in Israel! This one, though, is the tastiest!

Remember: *kneidlach* is not only for Jews! My non-Jewish mother made *kneidlach* every Passover, and all our Christian neighbours came to eat them and envied us because in communist Romania only the Jews (like my father) got *matzah* and *matzah* flour from the American Jewish Joint Distribution Committee.

Serves 10–14

2 eggs, beaten
90 ml (½ cup) sunflower oil
240 ml (1 cup) water
130 g (1 cup) *matzah* flour
salt and black pepper to taste
half a bunch parsley (without stalks), finely chopped

1. Mix all the ingredients well, then place the dough in the refrigerator for 30 minutes.
2. Boil water. Make 3 cm (just over 1 in) balls from the dough (wet your hands from time to time, because the mixture is sticky) and place them in the boiling water. Cook for 10 minutes.
3. To serve: place 2–3 kneidlach in a soup bowl and pour the soup over them.

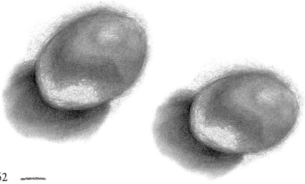

Summer stew (V)

This stew is a delicious mixture of vegetables and grains.

Serves 8–10

I recommend you use an iron pot.

The vegetable mix

4 medium onions, cut into quarters, or 2 leeks, cut into large pieces (or a mixture of both)

half a bulb of garlic cloves, peeled and cut into chunks

1 medium carrot, finely cut

2 celery stalks with leaves, chopped

1 sweet pepper (bell pepper), cut into strips

3 large tomatoes, cut into quarters

3 courgettes (zucchinis), thickly sliced

1 small butternut squash or summer pumpkin, peeled and cut into cubes

1 litre (4 cups) water or stock

80 ml (⅓ cup) soy sauce

120 ml (½ cup) olive oil

The grain mix

100 g (½ cup) brown rice

100 g (½ cup) oat groats

100 g (½ cup) pearl barley

50 g (¼ cup) black or red rice or millet

85 g (½ cup) quinoa

1. Place the vegetables in an iron pot and add the water or stock, soy sauce and oil.
2. Mix the grains and add them to the pot.
3. Bring the pot to the boil then lower the heat and simmer for an hour.

For those who prefer the vegetables to be more dominant, reduce the quantity of grains, and adjust the amount of water added. Or you could adjust the other way around: more of the grains and less of the vegetables.

You can also choose to add cooked chickpeas.

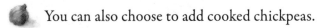 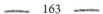

Hungarian steamed red cabbage (v)

In my childhood we had roast duck with mashed potato and steamed red cabbage for lunch every Sunday. Since then the duck has disappeared but the red cabbage is a permanent guest on my table at festive events!

Serves 8–10

sunflower oil for frying
1 small red cabbage (500 g or 1 lb)
60 ml ¼ cup water
3 tbs brown sugar
4 tbs apple cider vinegar
salt and black pepper to taste

1. Cut the cabbage in half, take out its heart (the white bit) while apologising, chop finely, place it in a pot with the oil and fry for 5–8 minutes. Stir occasionally.
2. Add the water, cover the pot and cook for 15–20 minutes, until the cabbage is soft. If needed add more water so the cabbage doesn't burn.
3. Take the pot off the heat and add sugar, vinegar, salt and pepper.

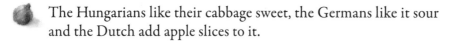 The Hungarians like their cabbage sweet, the Germans like it sour and the Dutch add apple slices to it.

Rich nut roast

I learnt this incredibly easy but delicious version of nut roast from Diana Greer, the mother of Helen, my dearest soul and spirit mate in England.

Makes 12 slices

You will need a loaf tin, 35 cm (14 in) in length.

Preheat oven to 180° C (350° F).

olive oil for sautéing
2 medium onions, finely chopped
2 medium carrots, grated
2 celery stalks with leaves, finely
 chopped
half a garlic clove, crushed
80 g (1 cup) oatmeal
500 g (1 lb) nut mix (hazelnut and
 walnut) roughly grated (so there will
 be something to bite on!) or finely
 grated (if you want a smooth roast)

75 g (½ cup) breadcrumbs or
 wholewheat flour or chickpea flour (if
 you need the roast to be gluten free)
2 tbs tomato paste
4 eggs, beaten
1 bunch parsley, chopped
salt and pepper

1. Sauté the onions in the olive oil until golden. Add the carrot, celery and garlic and steam on a low heat, with the lid on, until all the vegetables are soft. Take them off the heat.
2. Mix the oatmeal, nuts and breadcrumbs or wholewheat flour and add to the vegetable mix.
3. Add the tomato paste, eggs, parsley, salt and pepper. Stir.
4. Oil and line the loaf tin, pour the mixture into it and bake for 45 minutes.

 When serving, pour sweet and sour apple sauce (see below) on the slices.

Sweet and sour apple sauce (V)

This apple sauce is very good on nut roast and on almond burgers. It keeps well in a closed container. Do not freeze it unless you have no choice. (As a rule I do not eat frozen food, but I also believe that rules are there to be broken, so in emergencies I do use the freezer.)

Makes 1 ¹/₄ litres (2 ¹/₂ U.S. pints)

olive oil for sautéing
1 large onion, finely chopped
250 g (½ lb) green apples, coarsely grated unpeeled
75 g (⅓ cup) brown sugar
2–3 tbs balsamic vinegar
60 ml (¼ cup) soy sauce
500 ml (1 U.S. pints) water

Sauté the onions in the oil until brown. Add all the ingredients, bring to a boil and cook on a low heat for an hour.

You can blend it if you prefer a smooth texture!

Hungarian beetroot (beet) salad (V)

I recommend you make this one day before serving.

Serves 6–8

3 large beetroots (beets), washed } Cover the beetroots (beets) in water and cook for half an hour until soft, but not too soft. Cool and peel by hand. Grate, or finely slice, and place in a bowl.

The dressing

480 ml (2 cups) water
2 bay leaves
60 ml (¼ cup) apple cider vinegar
3 tbs brown sugar
1 tsp black pepper
2 tsp salt

} Boil the water. Add the rest of the ingredients to it, and cook for another 5 minutes. Pour the dressing over the beets.

1 tbs horseradish, grated } Add and mix. Keep refrigerated.

Almond and fruit tart

Serves 10–12

You will need a 26 cm (10 in) diameter pie or flan dish.
Preheat the oven to 180° C (350° F).

The pastry

125 g (4 ½ oz) very soft butter
3 tbs brown sugar
1 egg, beaten
190 g (1 ¼ cups) wholewheat flour

Mix in a bowl by hand until the pastry dough becomes unified. Place in the refrigerator for 20 minutes. Roll out the dough and line the oiled pie dish with it by pressing it to the bottom of the dish with your fingers.

The filling

1 kg (2 lb) fruit (apples, plumbs, apricots…),
  cut into medium-sized cubes
1 tbs cinnamon
4 tbs lemon juice

Mix and pour onto the chilled pastry shell.

The topping

150 g (5 oz) very soft butter
200 g (1 cup) brown sugar
3 tbs lemon peel, grated
3 eggs, beaten
150 g (5 oz) almonds or nuts, finely ground
1 ½ tbs wholewheat flour

Combine and spoon all over the fruit.

Bake for 10 minutes at 180° C (350° F). Lower the oven heat to 160° C (320° F) and keep baking for another 30 minutes.

Serve with vanilla sauce (see page 255), or home-made ice cream (see page 93).

Menus Through the Seasons

Cold days

MINESTRONE SOUP (V)

NETTLE, SPINACH AND SWISS CHARD QUICHE

CELERY ROOT SALAD

**ORANGE ALMOND CAKE
(THE FOUR-HUNDRED KILOMETRE CAKE)**

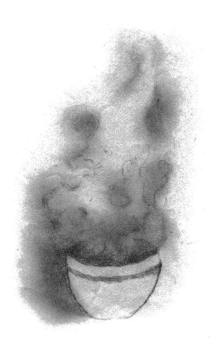

Minestrone soup (V)

Serves 12

When the days become cold and the hours of darkness lengthen, there is nothing more comforting than a rich, hot minestrone soup. It can be the centre of a lunch, with rye bread and spreads such as Hungarian givetch (see page 91), parsley and fresh coriander (cilantro) pesto (see page 138), and olive spread (see page 149). If you would like to eat something in addition, I recommend house salad or Greek salad. You can substitute other types of bread, like sourdough spelt bread or a simple mixed-grains bread.

200 g (1 cup) beans (any kind – red are harder than the others, so we usually use white)

Soak for 24 hours then cook for an hour or until soft. Save the cooking water and use it in the soup.

olive oil for sautéing
2 medium onions, chopped

} Sauté until golden.

3 celery stalks with leaves, finely chopped
1 red pepper, cubed
2 large carrots, sliced
quarter cauliflower, broken into florets
1 kohlrabi, diced, or 1 celeriac, diced

} Add to the onions and sauté for 5 minutes.

2 ½ litres (5 U.S. pints) stock or water
100 g (¾ cup) tomato paste
3 bay leaves

Add and cook until all the vegetables are soft. Turn off the heat.

1 large courgette (zucchini), finely sliced
3 tbs fresh basil, finely chopped
1 tbs dry oregano
2 tbs sugar
1 bunch parsley, finely chopped
salt and pepper to taste

Add and leave the lid on.

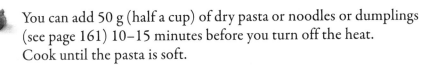

You can add 50 g (half a cup) of dry pasta or noodles or dumplings (see page 161) 10–15 minutes before you turn off the heat.
Cook until the pasta is soft.

Nettle, spinach and Swiss chard quiche

The nettle, which grows practically everywhere, is used in folk medicine to cure rheumatic pains. Every day my Omama (my grandmother), who suffered from rheumatism, would ask me to pick a bunch for her. I went out into the fields surrounding our house and picked them wearing gloves. My grandmother would hold the bunch in her bare hands and hit her aching knees with it. They would swell up and become red but she felt relief from her pain.

Nettle is a curative herb that is beneficial for the blood system. When drunk as tea it can lower blood pressure. It also contains iron. My father, who was taken to a work camp in Russia during the Second World War, told me that two things saved him while he was there: garlic and nettles.

In the height of the Israeli winter, a variety of green leaves emerge from the depth of the earth. Bedouin women from the area can be seen daily picking many different kinds. I always want to learn from them their built-in knowledge of nature's wisdom. Like nettles, wild spinach can easily be found.

Do not be afraid to pick nettles with your bare hands – it is good for inflamed joints and rheumatism. By the time the quiche is ready, you will no longer feel the stinging, and the healing powers of the nettle will already be absorbed in your body.

You will need a 28 cm (11 in) diameter pie dish.
Preheat oven to 150° C (300° F).

Serves 10–12

The pastry

75 g (2 ½ oz) very soft butter
40 g (¼ cup) sesame seeds
2 tbs linseeds
75 g (½ cup) wholewheat flour
25 g (⅓ cup) oatmeal
3 tbs water
pinch of salt

Mix by hand in a bowl until a dough comes together. Place in the oiled pie dish, press with your fingers to the bottom of the dish.

The filling

olive oil for sautéing

4 large onions or 4 large leeks, finely chopped

6 garlic cloves, crushed

600 g (1 ¼ lb) fresh green leaves (if you don't live in the country and have no access
  to nettle or wild spinach, use regular spinach and Swiss chard)

200 g (7 oz) feta cheese, crumbled

250 ml (1 cup) yogurt

3 eggs, beaten

pinch black pepper

sunflower or pumpkin seeds

1. Wash the green leaves well. Make sure any dirt or grit is rinsed away.
    Put them into a pot with a tiny bit of water, cook with the lid on for 2–3
    minutes, until they are wilted but not overcooked. Drain, cool and chop.
2. Sauté the onions or leeks until golden. Add garlic, stir and sauté 2 minutes
    more. Take off the heat.
3. Add the green leaves, cheese, yogurt, eggs and black pepper to the onions
    or leeks. Mix.
4. Pour the filling into the pie dish onto the waiting pressed dough. Sprinkle
    sunflower seeds or pumpkin seeds on the top.
5. Bake for 45–60 minutes.

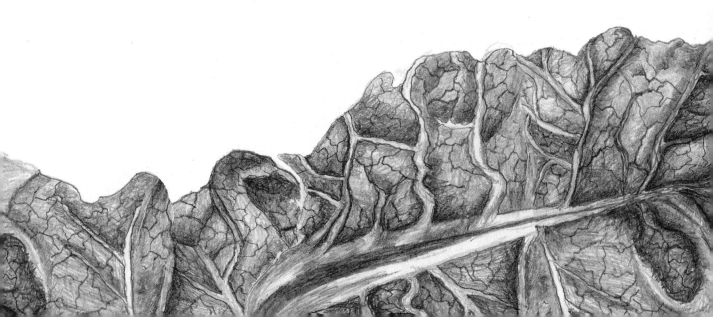

Celeriac salad

This salad is tastier if you make it one day before serving.

Serves 4–6

  1 large celeriac, roughly grated
  2 gherkins (pickled cucumbers), finely sliced
  2 tbs dry white wine
  5 tbs olive oil
  juice of half a lemon
  2–3 tbs sour cream
  salt and pepper

Mix all the ingredients in a bowl.

Instead of the wine, olive oil and lemon juice, you can add Roquefort dressing (see page 58)

The four-hundred kilometre cake

Living in England had many advantages: the cold weather, which I prefer to the heat; long walks in the countryside; trips to Wales, Scotland, the Lake District and Cornwall, all of which connected me to the books I had read in my youth and the Jane Austen films I would later see. But it also had a great disadvantage: eating out in restaurants was a nightmare. The pubs' meat-oriented offerings and the lack of wholesomeness of restaurant fare left me with a constant hunger for good food.

So my heart leaped with expectation when, returning from a hike in the south-west corner of England, we passed through Dorchester, a small town 400 kilometres (about 250 miles) from where we lived, and I saw a sign on the main street: Ciao Café. 'That sounds Italian,' I said to Helen, my Australian housemate. She and her son, William, together with my son, Adam, were all dozing in the car. 'Maybe there's good food here.'

Well, good food we didn't find. The ravioli tasted suspiciously like frozen pasta, the pizza was soggy, the salad poor and tasteless. But the cakes, my God, looked terrific. Out of the wide choice (which always leaves me with the feeling that I have not chosen the right one), we finally decided on the orange almond cake. It sounded exotic and was a totally

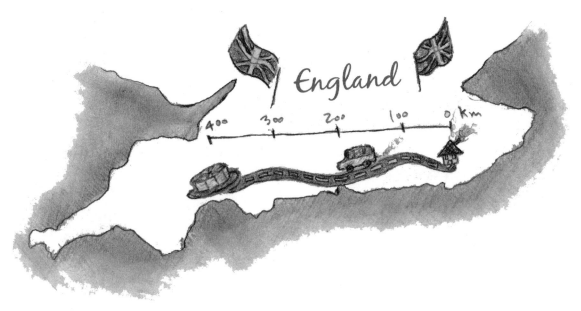

new taste combination for me. After the first bite I put down my fork, closed my eyes and gave in to the pleasure of sweetness, bitterness and sourness uniting in my mouth.

In spite of having grown up on the exquisite delights in Hungarian bakery cafés – *Dobos torta*, *Eszterházy torta*, chestnut purée with whipped cream – this cake was definitely the best cake I had ever tasted. My Israeli chutzpah (cheeky confidence) prompted me to ask for the owner of the café, who turned out to be a young Italian baker married to an English woman. He sat down with us and we exchanged stories about different foods. His openness and kindness filled me with hope and I dared to ask for the great cake's recipe. His face became serious as he informed me that he never shared recipes. Even my argument that we lived 400 kilometres away and so would certainly not open a café next to his did not help. In spite of my great disappointment, we parted as friends.

But I never forgot that orange almond cake. A few months later, I woke up one Saturday morning with the clear certainty that on that day I would eat that cake. Again, it was not difficult to convince my adventurous housemate to join me. So there we were, with the boys, heading to Dorchester, 400 kilometres away. By then I had totally let go of getting the recipe, but the expectation of eating that heavenly cake filled me with joy. The taste was just as marvellous as before. Our baker recognised us and came to greet us. We chatted as old friends. At the end of our visit, we had almost left when he returned to us with a piece of paper in his hand. 'Here is the cake's recipe,' he said, to my great surprise. 'Someone who travels 400 kilometres for a slice of cake is worthy to receive it.'

When I began running Harduf's restaurant in Israel and the first customer asked me for a recipe, I decided on the spot to share all my recipes with my customers. 'I am honoured if you want to cook my food in your home,' I said to them. We were both happy. In my heart I thanked my Italian baker.

Orange almond cake (the four-hundred kilometre cake)

Serves 12–14

You will need a round, 28 cm (11 in) diameter cake tin.
Preheat oven to 180° C (350° F).

2 medium oranges with thin peel
6 eggs
330 g (3 cups) ground almonds (if the almonds are bleached, the cake comes out
 melting in your mouth; if unbleached, it is still delicious but with more of a "body")
250 g (1 ¼ cups) brown sugar

1. Cook the oranges (with their peel on) for 20 minutes in water that covers
    them. Cool, cut into four, take out the pips and blend very well, either in a
    food processor or in a blender.
2. Separate the eggs. Beat the whites with 50 g (¼ cup) of the sugar, until
    very stiff.
3. Beat (with the same beaters) the egg yolks with the rest of the sugar (200 g
    1 cup), until they become light. Add the blended oranges and the almonds.
    Mix well.
4. Fold in the egg whites and mix gently until you get an even texture.
5. Grease and line the cake tin. Pour the cake into it and bake at 180° C (350° F),
    for approximately 1 hour. If you see that the top is becoming brown but the
    body is still really wobbly, cover the top with baking paper and reduce the
    heat to 160° C (320° F). Bake until the cake is firm. Note that this is a very
    soft and light cake, so it isn't possible to put a thin knife into it to check
    whether it's ready – the knife will never come out clean. Even when ready,
    the cake will be moist! I am warning you that determining the baking time
    requires attention and actual touching!

The cake tastes heavenly served warm or cooled.

Vanilla cream (see page 255) goes beautifully with it.

Hot days

In this meal there are lots of dairy ingredients and thus it suits Shavuot, a Jewish festival that is celebrated in early summer, and in which we eat lots of cheeses. Shavuot is a time of new community and meeting together.

CHEESE AND VEGETABLE PIE

BUTTERNUT SQUASH STUFFED WITH VEGETABLES, QUINOA AND PINE NUTS (V)

HOUSE SALAD WITH FRENCH DRESSING (SEE PAGES 84 AND 59)

GREEN BEAN SALAD (V)

YOGURT AND CUCUMBER SOUP

BERRY AND VANILLA RICE PUDDING TRIFLE

Cheese and vegetable pie

This is a most delicious pie; you will love it!

Serves 10–12

You will need a 28 cm (11 in) diameter pie dish or a rectangular tin, 23 x 35 cm (9 x 14 in).
Preheat the oven to 150° C (300° F).

The pastry

75 g (2 ½ oz) very soft butter
40 g (¼ cup) sesame seeds
2 tbs linseeds
75 g (½ cup) wholewheat flour
25 g (⅓ cup) oatmeal
3 tbs water
pinch of salt

Mix by hand in a bowl until the dough comes together well. Place in the oiled pie dish, press with your fingers to the bottom of the dish.

The filling

olive oil for sautéing
2 large leeks, washed and chopped,
    or 4 large onions, chopped

Sauté until golden.

200 g (7 oz) mushrooms, sliced
1 red pepper, cut into strips

Add and sauté for 5 minutes.
Put in a big bowl.

Continues

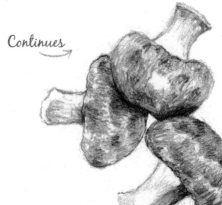

180 ml (¾ cup) yogurt or single (light) cream
    or coconut milk
375 g (13 oz) cheese (feta, hard white cheese,
    ricotta, Roquefort – either one or two of
    these; vegans can use grated tofu)
a handful of fresh basil, chopped
4 eggs, beaten (or, for vegans, 1 tbs linseed,
    crushed, and mixed with 2 tbs water)
pumpkin or sunflower seeds

Mix and add to the bowl of the vegetables.

Pour into the pie dish, sprinkle sunflower seeds or pumpkin seeds on top and bake for 50 minutes until it gets some colour on top.

 According to your mood, desire or situation in the refrigerator, use other vegetables instead of mushrooms and peppers, such as steamed broccoli, thickly sliced courgette (zucchini), steamed cauliflower florets or finely chopped Swiss chard or spinach.

Butternut squash stuffed with vegetables, quinoa and pine nuts (V)

Butternut squash is a summer fruit. She grows out of a beautiful flower just as her brothers and sisters – pumpkins, squashes, courgettes (zucchinis) and cucumbers – do. At the edge where the flower is connected to the plant, a gradually growing 'belly' starts to emerge. In the end, this baby fruit totally devours the flower, just as our newborn babies do in a soul way to us mothers.

Serves 6

Preheat oven to 150° C (300° F).

Start by cooking the 2 cups quinoa or mixed grains (see page 68–69).

The filling

    olive oil for sautéing
    3 medium onions, finely chopped
    1 small leek, finely chopped
    1 red pepper (bell pepper), small cubes
    1 celery stalk with leaves, finely chopped
    4–5 mushrooms, finely sliced

Sauté the onions and leek until golden. Add the pepper (bell pepper), celery and mushrooms and sauté for another 5 minutes. Turn off the heat.

    400 g (2 cups) cooked quinoa or mixed grains
    30 g (¼ cup) pine nuts, or chopped pecans, lightly toasted
    pinch of finely grated nutmeg
    a handful of fresh basil, chopped
    pinch of salt

Add and mix.

The sauce

480 ml (2 cups) single (light) cream or coconut milk
180 ml (¾ cup) soy and honey sauce (see page 118)

Mix.

Stuffing the butternuts

3 medium butternut squashes (1.5 kg, approximately 3 lb)

1. Cut the butternut squashes lengthwise into two. Take out the seeds.
2. Steam in a little water for 15–20 minutes in a covered pot, until the squash is soft but not too soft.
3. Spoon out some of the flesh of the squash, leaving a finger-width thickness around the squash shell. Add the spooned out flesh to the filling, or to a soup!
4. Fill the butternut squash shell with the filling and put in a baking pan or tray.
5. Pour the sauce on the squashes. Bake for 15–20 minutes.
6. It is advisable to leave some of the sauce for serving since all the sauce you pour on the squashes will be absorbed during the baking.

Green bean salad (V)

Serves 6–8

Make a few hours in advance of serving.

The marinade

  1 tbs soy sauce
  ½ tsp Dijon mustard
  4 tbs olive oil
  1–2 tbs balsamic vinegar

Mix.

  400 g (14 oz) green beans or broad beans, topped and tailed
  1 red pepper (bell pepper), cubed
  1–2 garlic cloves, crushed
  salt and pepper

Steam the beans in little water or in a steamer. They should stay crunchy! Cool them. Put them in a bowl.
  Add the other ingredients and then the marinade. Mix well and let it sit for a few hours before serving, so the vegetables can 'drink' the marinade in.

 You can sprinkle toasted sesame seeds on top.

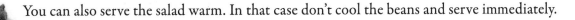 You can also serve the salad warm. In that case don't cool the beans and serve immediately.

Yogurt and cucumber soup

Specially nice on hot days!

Make a few hours in advance of serving.

Serves 4–6

5 medium cucumbers, roughly grated
1 litre (2 U.S. pints) yogurt (see page 62)
2 garlic cloves, crushed
large handful of fresh mint, chopped
2 tsp salt
5 tbs olive oil

Mix and put in the refrigerator a few hours before serving.

When serving, sprinkle chopped spring onions (scallions) and sweet paprika on top. Then you get three colours: green, white and red.

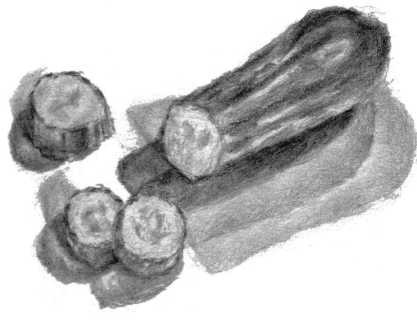

Berry and vanilla rice pudding trifle

I love this dessert from the days of my childhood. In Budapest's famous cafés it is served in a tall elegant glass and displayed in a glass-fronted fridge, so everyone who sees it will definitely want to put their spoon in it. The dessert is composed of layers of white rice (no guilty feelings, please!) cooked in milk, berry fruit salad, vanilla sauce (see page 255) and cream.

You will need a tall glass for each person.

Serves 8–10

Rice in milk

240 ml (1 cup) water
480 ml (2 cups) milk
} Bring to the boil.

200 g (1 cup) white rice
150 g (¾ cup) brown sugar
} Add and simmer on low heat for 30 minutes. Stir from time to time. If the rice 'resists' softening, add more milk and cook until soft (this rice loves to burn on the bottom – be aware). Cool.

1 tsp vanilla essence (extract)
} Add at the end.

Berry fruits

150 g (1 cup) strawberries, sliced
150 g (1 cup) blueberries
150 g (1 cup) raspberries
} Mix.

Continues

Assembling the trifle

1 quantity vanilla sauce (see page 255)
whipping cream
2 tsp sugar

1. Put the rice in milk at the bottom of each tall glass.
2. Pour vanilla sauce onto the rice.
3. Tip berries gently onto the vanilla sauce.
4. Top with cream whipped with 2 tsp sugar.

 You could, of course, eat just the berries as a dessert in themselves with vanilla sauce or whipped cream.

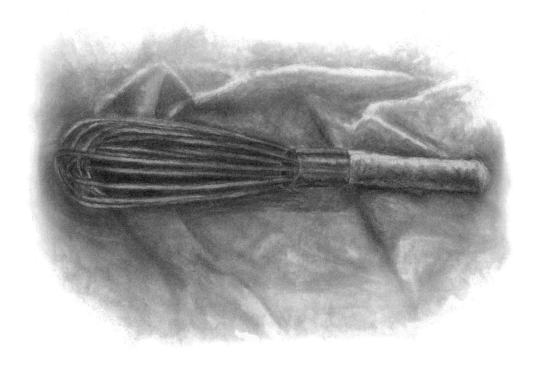

Raspberries

On a bright July morning I went raspberry picking in the Golan Heights. What a different experience this was from being in Mother's raspberry garden in Transylvania! In the Golan, raspberries are cultivated, all hanging in orderly rows, the fruit easily reachable. The only effort one has to make is bending down to pick the berries that hide at the bottom of the bushes.

Mother's raspberry garden was one square plot, bushes close together all higgledy-piggledy. Entering it was like penetrating a tropical jungle with no path between the bushes. Getting close to gather the berries, I suffered many scratches from the thin but persistent thorns, while hundreds of mosquitoes fed on my blood and an army of spiders attacked my flesh. Yet the heavenly taste of the raspberries made me forget everything in the world and I just ate and ate and ate. But in the evening the scratches and mosquito bites emerged to torture me through the night. Nevertheless, the next day I was drawn back to the thorny bushes, starting again the cycle of indulgence and suffering.

I cannot say I did not have a great time in the Golan Heights. In fact I spent four hours there without noticing where the time flew. The raspberries were delicious and since they were not sprayed with chemicals they reminded me of Mother's berries. Yet when I returned home I felt that something was missing.

The scratches and the bites?

A Menu Celebrating Salads

A Menu Celebrating Salads

BEAN AND CHICKPEA SALAD (V)

RICH LEAFY SALAD WITH ROQUEFORT DRESSING

COLOURFUL ROASTED PEPPERS (BELL PEPPERS) SALAD (V)

CORN BREAD

ALMOND PATÉ

QUINOA AND MILLET TABBOULEH (V)

BASIL AND PINE NUT PESTO

SUMMERY FRUIT SALAD (V)

SPECIAL LEMONADE (V)

Bean and chickpea salad (v)

Begin this salad three days before eating. One day is needed for soaking, one day for sprouting and a third day in which the prepared salad stands in the refrigerator. But if you are short of time, it still tastes good if you soak it on one day, then skip the sprouting stage to cook and prepare it the next.

Serves 8–10

200 g (1 cup) red kidney beans with 700 ml (3 cups) water for soaking
200 g (1 cup) chickpeas with 700 ml (3 cups) water for soaking
2 more litres (4 U.S. pints) water for cooking

1. Soak the pulses separately for 24 hours.
2. Drain the water and leave the pulses (still separate) in sieves (strainers) for 24 hours to start the germinating process. From time to time sprinkle water on them.
3. Cook the pulses in another 2 litres (4 U.S. pints) water (1 litre – 2 U.S. pints – each) until they are soft (minimum 60–90 minutes). Keep them separate, as they will take different amounts of time to cook.
4. Drain, cool and mix them together in a bowl.

1–2 carrots, finely sliced or cut into cubes
1 celery stalk (without leaves!), finely chopped
half a bunch spring onion (scallions), chopped
half a bunch parsley, finely chopped

} Add to the pulses in the bowl.

The marinade

60 ml (⅓ cup) olive oil
5 tbs apple cider vinegar
4 garlic cloves, crushed
1 tbs Dijon mustard
salt and pepper to taste

Mix and pour onto the beans and vegetables. Combine well, so the marinade covers all the ingredients.

Keep in a cold place for a day before serving.

olives
tomatoes, sliced

Decorate with olives and sliced tomatoes on top just before serving.

Rich leafy salad with Roquefort dressing

Roquefort dressing has a creamy texture. It is suitable for a simple meal that does not have especially exotic flavours, served with a rich leaf salad.

Serves 6–8

a variety of leaves, or half a lettuce, broken into large chunks
1 bunch of rocket (arugula), torn up a little
3–4 mustard leaves, finely chopped

Roquefort dressing (see page 58)

1 fruit (apple, pear, plum, orange or peach) cut into cubes
30 g (¼ cup) walnuts, chopped and toasted
large handful of croutons (see page 84) (optional)

1. Put all the leaves in a bowl.
2. Pour the dressing onto the leaves minutes before serving.
3. Decorate the salad with the fruit, the nuts and the croutons.
4. Bring it to the table and, after your guests' eyes have finished admiring God's rich creation, toss and serve.

Colourful roasted peppers (bell peppers) salad (V)

Serves 4–6

Preheat oven to 160° C (320° F).

4–6 peppers (red, yellow and green bell peppers), cut into thick strips
6 tbs olive oil
3 garlic cloves, crushed
2 tbs balsamic vinegar
½ tbs honey
2 tbs soy sauce

1. Put the peppers in a baking dish, pour the oil over them and bake for 15 minutes, until they get some light brown colour.
2. Tip the peppers into a bowl, add the rest of the ingredients and mix.

feta or any other white hard cheese, cubed
or tofu cubes marinated for 15 minutes in water and soy sauce

3. Just before serving the salad, add cheese or tofu cubes.

Corn bread

I don't normally usually use baking powder, but this bread needs it for rising.

You will need a loaf tin, 35 cm (14 in) in length, greased and lined.

Preheat the oven to 150° C (300° F).

Simple corn bread

170 g (1 cup) yellow cornmeal
110 g (¾ cup) wholewheat flour
2 tsp baking powder
pinch of salt

Mix in a bowl.

3 eggs, beaten
240 ml (1 cup) yogurt
60 ml (¼ cup) sunflower oil
45 ml (¼ cup) honey

Mix in a separate bowl. Then add to the flour mixture and combine well. Put the dough in the oiled loaf tin, bake for 30–40 minutes.

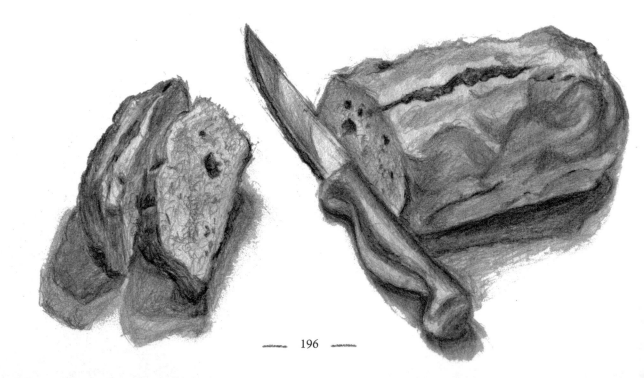

Cheese and onion corn bread

170 g (1 cup) yellow cornmeal
150 g (1 cup) wholewheat flour
3 tsp baking powder
half a tsp salt

Mix.

1 egg, beaten
240 ml (1 cup) yogurt
2 tbs honey

Mix in a separate bowl, add to the flour mixture and mix well.

1 onion, chopped
olive oil for sautéing
150 g (1 cup) cooked sweetcorn
60 g (½ cup) yellow cheese, grated

Sauté the onion in the oil until golden. Add the golden onion with the sweetcorn and cheese to the dough. Combine well.

Put the dough in the oiled loaf tin and bake for 30–40 minutes.

Almond paté

Serves 10
Makes approx 750 ml (3–4 cups)

Start by hard boiling 2 eggs.

170 g (1 cup) almonds	Roast in the oven for 8–10 minutes at 150° C (300° F).
olive oil for sautéing 3 large onions, chopped	Sauté until very soft and golden.
2 hard-boiled eggs, shelled salt and pepper	Put all the ingredients in a food processor to blend them into paté.

Serve with crackers, rice cakes or bread.

Quinoa and millet tabbouleh (v)

Tabbouleh is a Middle-Eastern salad that combines hearty grain with fresh, zesty flavours. This dish also goes wonderfully well with almond burgers, pies or stir-fried vegetables with tofu.

Serves 6–8

175 g (1 cup) quinoa
100 g (½ cup) millet
540 ml (2 ¼ cups) water

Cook on low heat 30–40 minutes until the grains are fluffy and the water is absorbed. Add more water if it absorbs too quickly and the grains are still hard. Cool and put in a bowl.

2 tomatoes, cubed
2 cucumbers, cut into half-finger-width sticks
half a bunch spring onion (scallions), chopped
juice of a lemon
4 garlic cloves, crushed
olive oil
fresh basil or mint leaves or parsley, chopped
salt and pepper

Add to the bowl. Mix.

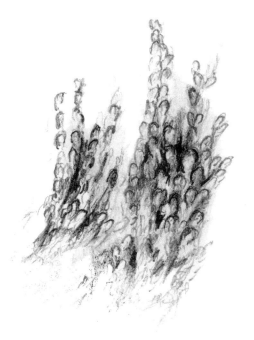

Basil and pine nut pesto

Makes about 500 g (1 lb)

200 g (7 oz) pine nuts
2 cups fresh basil leaves
4 garlic cloves
180 g (1 cup) parmesan cheese, grated
180 ml (1 cup) olive oil

Blend all ingredients except the olive oil in a food processor. Add olive oil gradually, stopping when you have a good, smooth consistency. Eat immediately on bread or crackers or rice cakes. Store in a jar in the refrigerator. Use on pasta.

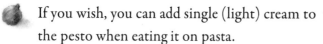 If you wish, you can add single (light) cream to the pesto when eating it on pasta.

Summery fruit salad (v)

Fruit salad is usually thought of as dessert, but in fact it is healthier to eat fruit as the first course. Fruit breaks down more quickly than other food and if we eat it at the end of a meal it is forced to wait its 'turn' to be absorbed in the digestive system, so it ferments and therefore strains the digestive process.

Serves 6–8

  2 large ripe mangos, cubed
  1 bunch black grapes, stems and pips removed
  1 small melon, cubed
  1 plum, cubed
  4 tbs concentrated apple juice
  1 tbs runny honey (optional)

Mix in a bowl.

You can serve this with yogurt, and granola
(see page 230) sprinkled on top.

Special lemonade (v)

Makes 2 litres (4 U.S. pints)

150 g (¾ cup) brown sugar
a few leaves of lemongrass, melissa or lemon verbena
juice of 2–3 lemons
1 ½ litres (3 U.S. pints) cold water
1 lemon, cut in four, pips removed

1. Put the sugar and leaves in a pot, add water that covers them and boil until the sugar melts. Cool.
2. In a jug, mix the above cooled liquid, lemon juice and cold water.
3. Crush the lemon in a blender, with its peel. Add it to the lemonade, tasting as you go to ensure a balance between sweetness and sharpness.

Indian Menu

Although I have never been to India, I love Indian food. With the help of an Indian family who have a spice shop in a nearby town, I have learned to make several dishes that have become my favourites.

Indian restaurants and Indian food are not common in Romania or Israel.

A real vegetarian Indian dinner is composed of many small dishes, in the centre of which is rice, dhal (lentils) and curried vegetables. These are usually accompanied by chapati – thin Indian bread (I do not include chapati in my menu because eating rice and wheat in the same meal fills up space in the stomach that could be taken by something more nourishing, like fresh salad); chutney – a sort of jam made with spices; raita – yogurt with cucumber or fruit; and poppadoms – thin crisps made from chickpea flour, which I buy at the Indian shop.

For me this version, as it is not excruciatingly spicy, is a perfect meal and I can eat it day after day.

Still, if I'm being honest with you, I have to warn you about my Indian meal!

Once an elderly Indian lady entered the restaurant dressed in a beautiful sari (in Israel this is quite an unusual sight) and I said to Fatma and Keren (the team) that I hoped she would not choose the Indian meal. She studied the menu for a long time and finally did choose the Indian meal. I tried to persuade her to go for our varied and extremely delicious other meals, but she was rock-solid in her choice.

Shaking a little, I served her the curry. When she had finished eating, I cleared her table and, more out of politeness than boldness, I asked her opinion of it. She looked at me and said, 'Your Indian curry was delicious.' And as I was walking away she added with a big smile, 'It was a little bit Hungarian.' So now you know what you will get in this chapter!

Indian meal

HOME-MADE CURRY POWDER (V)

SPICED RICE (V)

FRAGRANT LENTILS (DAHL) (V)

PIQUANT CHICKPEA CURRY

CURRIED VEGETABLES IN COCONUT MILK (V)

APPLE CHUTNEY (V)

RAITA

POPPADOMS

The copper mortar

A few years ago I took Mother's copper mortar with me to Israel and used it as a decorative item in my kitchen. In my childhood there were no electric grinders so we put spice seeds into this mortar and, by hitting them hard with a round-edged handle, we transformed them into powder. But during the latter years the mortar had become dustier and dustier because my family either bought ground spices or used a shiny white electric grinder.

One day the sad golden object on my shelf caught my eye, and I decided to return the mortar to its true task. I put a few small black peppercorns in it and started hitting them. In the beginning they united against me, not willing to share the secret of their essence, and stubbornly staying hard.

My thoughts roamed to the world of only six-hundred years ago when India and the Far East had not yet been discovered by European traders. My favourite spices, like cardamom seeds, cumin seeds, turmeric, ginger root, peppercorns, mustard seeds and coriander seeds, did not exist in European kitchens. Once the merchants started to bring them by land or by sea, brave cooks began to experiment with the new tastes. Different worlds united in people's stomachs.

Today, merchants do not have to fear robbers attacking caravans loaded with expensive spices. And all we have to do is go to the closest Indian shop.

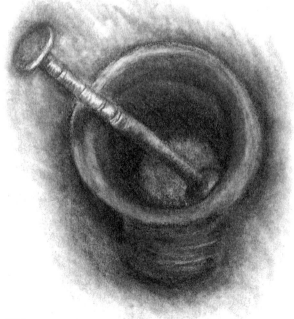

The peppercorns are surrendering to my determined rhythmical movements. Their hard roundness transforms into powder, their blackness turns to grey. And the mortar is shining.

Home-made curry powder (V)

This spice mixture keeps for a long time in a well-closed jar. The suggested quantity is suitable for lovers of Indian food who plan to use the mixture frequently in their cooking. Those who rarely cook Indian food should prepare a quarter of the quantity.

5 tbs cardamom seeds
5 tbs coriander seeds
5 tbs cumin seeds

Toast on low heat, stirring constantly, for 15 minutes. Turn off the heat.

1 ½ tbs dark mustard seeds

Add to the toasted seeds and grind to a fine powder.

1 ¼ tbs ginger powder
1 ¼ tbs cinnamon
2 ½ tbs turmeric

Add and mix well. Store in a closed jar.

Spiced rice (V)

5 tbs olive oil for frying
¾ tsp anise seeds
¾ tsp coriander seeds
4 cardamom seeds
570 g (3 cups) whole basmati rice
1 tbs salt
1 tsp turmeric
¾ tsp dry ginger
1 ½ litres (6 cups) water

Lightly heat the oil, add the anise, coriander
and cardamom. Stir constantly for half a minute.
Add the other spices and rice, stir well and
add the water. Bring to the boil. Lower heat,
cover pot and cook for 1 hour or until the
rice is cooked.

Fragrant lentils (Dahl) (V)

Serves 8–10

400 g (2 cups) lentils (red, black or green), washed and drained
1 ½ litres (3 U.S. pints) water

} Cook for 30–40 minutes on low heat, until lentils become soft. Take it off the heat.

sunflower oil for frying
4 or 5 medium onions, finely chopped
8 garlic cloves, crushed

} Fry the onions in plenty of oil on a medium heat, until golden. Add garlic.

1 tbs cumin seeds
1 tbs black mustard seeds

} Add to the onions and keep frying for 2 minutes.

half a bunch fresh coriander (cilantro), chopped
salt to taste
chilli powder to taste (start small and add!)

} Add the spices and onions to the lentils. Stir.

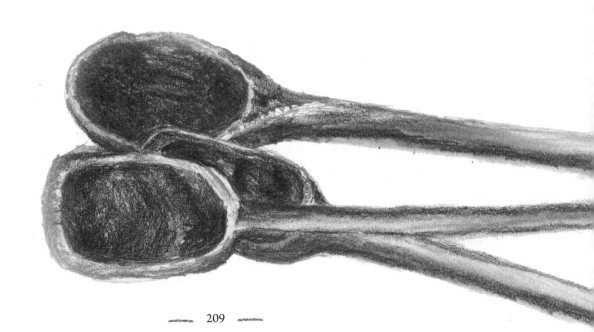

Piquant chickpea curry

Preparation for this dish ideally begins two days before the meal with soaking and sprouting the chickpeas. But soaking them one day beforehand is enough.

Serves 8–10

200 g (1 cup) chickpeas
480 ml (2 cups) water

Soak overnight. If you have time, drain and then sprout for 1 day (see page 64). Cook in water until soft. Keep the water.

olive oil for sautéing
3 large onions, finely chopped
8 garlic cloves, crushed

Sauté until the onion is golden. Add the garlic.

1 tsp cardamom seeds, ground
1 tbs turmeric powder
1 tsp cumin seeds
6 cloves

Add to the onion and sauté 2–3 minutes while stirring.

4 large tomatoes, cubed

Add to the onion mix and sauté 5 minutes.

Then add the cooked chickpeas with half a cup of their cooking water, and bring to the boil.

3 tbs tomato paste
1 tbs salt
chilli pepper, finely sliced, according to
  your endurance

Add tomato paste and salt and simmer for 5 minutes. Add chilli pepper. (Start with a small amount!)

150 g (⅔ cup) yogurt

Stir in after you have turned the heat off. Remove the cloves.

Curried vegetables in coconut milk (V)

Serves 8–10

sunflower oil for sautéing
3 medium onions, quartered
1 leek, chopped to big chunks
} Sauté in a big pot until golden.

2 tbs curry powder (see page 207) } Add and stir.

8 celery stalks with their leaves, chopped
4 medium carrots, thickly cut
2 red peppers, sliced
1 kohlrabi, cubed
} Add and cook for 2 minutes.

120 ml (½ cup) water
400 ml (14 U.S. fl oz) coconut milk
} Pour in. Cover, simmer on low heat for 15 minutes, stirring from time to time.

2 medium sweet potatoes, cubed
half a cauliflower, broken into florets
salt to taste
chilli (optional)
} Add and cook for 15 minutes. Stir occasionally.

1 large courgette (zucchini), cut into chunks } Add and cook for 5 minutes.

1 bunch fresh coriander (cilantro), chopped } Add after you have turned off the heat. Stir.

Apple chutney (V)

This is a sort of concentrated sweet-and-sour jam, an addition to the Indian kitchen that can be served with any Indian dish. It will keep for a long time in the refrigerator. While the chutney is cooking, the kitchen is filled with the strange smell of the onion and vinegar being cooked together. Do not be alarmed, the final result is really delicious!

There are many kinds of chutneys made from different fruits. This apple version is my favourite.

Serves 8–12

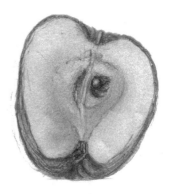

2 large onions, finely chopped
500 g (1 lb) apples, small cubes
150 g (1 ½ cups) brown sugar
¼ tsp ginger powder
pinch of chilli powder
40 g (¼ cup) raisins
1 ½ tsp salt
80 ml (⅓ cup) apple cider vinegar

Put all the ingredients into a pot, cook on medium heat for 1 ½ hours, stir occasionally. Store in a jar in the refrigerator.

Raita

Raita's task is to cool the spiciness of the meal.

Serves 8–10

3 large cucumbers, roughly grated
360 ml (1 ½ cups) yogurt
1 tsp cumin seeds, toasted and ground
½ tsp salt
chilli powder (optional)
2 tbs fresh mint, finely chopped

Mix all the ingredients and serve in a deep bowl.

Poppadoms

The poppadom is a wafer-thin, round, crispy Indian cracker – the Indian version of nachos. You can buy them in a shop that sells Indian food. Consult the shop assistant because some varieties are very spicy!

Fry without oil for one minute in a frying pan or skillet, turning it over often. In our restaurant we use tongs to hold the poppadom directly above the heat.

Indians place a small amount of rice on the poppadom, then add lentils, curried vegetables, chutney and raita, and eat it with their hands.

Home-made Biscuits, Cookies, Slices

Home-made Biscuits, Cookies, Slices

CAROB CAKE

CAROB BALLS

CAROB COOKIES

ALMOND BISCUITS

HAZELNUT AND LEMON SLICE

GINGER BISCUITS

COCONUT AND OATMEAL COOKIES

TAHINI BISCUITS

OAT, RAISIN AND WALNUT COOKIES

BLINTZES (HUNGARIAN PANCAKES)

SWEET TOPPINGS FOR BLINTZES OR PANCAKES

RICH GRANOLA (V)

 'Biscuit' here is British usage. North Americans would say 'cookie'.

Balancing our sugar consumption

In previous times human beings consumed sugar by eating honey that was produced from the nectar of flowers (with the help of bees, of course). This sugar was connected to flowers, and so also to the human digestive and reproductive systems. It nourished the forces of the human will.

In time, humans discovered sugar cane and started to produce cane sugar. Sugar cane is a stalk, which is related to the human rhythmic system and to the life of feeling.

In our times, sugar is extracted from sugar beets, which is a root. It is connected to the head and nourishes human thought. Modern human beings live mostly in their thoughts and in their head.

For strong health and a good life we need to create a balance between willing, feeling and thought. Nourishment can help to create this balance.

At the beginning of their lives, our children live in their will system and afterwards in their emotional system. The phenomenon of 'sophisticated' and 'intellectualised' children, who are more developed in their head than their souls can carry at their young age, is widespread in our times. Our children know too much, are unnecessarily bombarded with adult information, and have weak will forces as a result of not being involved in activities that connect them to the elements of the Earth. They spend far too much time from too early an age in front of the television and computer, developing passivity and getting stuck in their heads because they are processing thoughts instead of playing outside, walking in rain puddles and experiencing nature.

Eating an excess of sugar, especially sugar that has been extracted from sugar beets, encourages the thought processes of children and does not help them achieve balance. I strongly advise restricting the consumption of this kind of sugar, mostly for children, but also for parents. Accustom your children to low sugar consumption of every kind. If you want to make something sweet, use honey, as this supports life forces and will forces.

It is better to accustom your children to not eating sugar from the beginning, so that their basic sense of taste will not be 'ruined' by the sweetness. Sugar is not good, even if it's brown and organic. It disrupts the body's natural balance, which always has two spoons of sugar in the blood. Imagine what happens to this gentle balance if a child eats another spoon of sugar or sucks on a sugar candy.

On the other hand, everyone needs something sweet every now and again. Dessert after a Friday night meal or on festivals and birthdays is a reasonable habit. Just do not turn it into a daily habit. In this next section you are going to be exposed to many recipes for sweets. In fact this whole book has many desserts made with sugar. I put them in the book because I hope that if you give your kids and yourselves something sweet, it will usually be something home-made!

Carob cake

This cake is used to make carob balls (see next page) but it is also very tasty as a simple cake. For the indulgers: cover it with Omama's chocolate cream (see page 123). For the health freaks: use carob powder in the cream instead of cocoa powder.

You will need a round, 26 cm (10 in) diameter sprung cake tin.
Preheat oven to 150° C (300° F). Grease and line the cake tin.

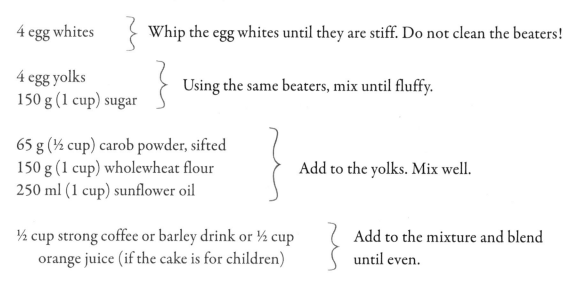

4 egg whites — Whip the egg whites until they are stiff. Do not clean the beaters!

4 egg yolks
150 g (1 cup) sugar — Using the same beaters, mix until fluffy.

65 g (½ cup) carob powder, sifted
150 g (1 cup) wholewheat flour
250 ml (1 cup) sunflower oil — Add to the yolks. Mix well.

½ cup strong coffee or barley drink or ½ cup orange juice (if the cake is for children) — Add to the mixture and blend until even.

Add the final yolk mixture to the whipped egg whites, folding gently. Pour the mixture into the greased tin. Bake for 35 minutes, until a knife stuck into the baked cake comes out clean.

Carob balls

Makes about 25 large balls or 50–60 small balls.

1 carob cake (see previous page)
120 g (1 cup) simple biscuits (plain sweet crackers), finely crushed
50 g (⅓ cup) raisins
60 ml (¼ cup) rum (optional) (Use a real rum!)
30 g (¼ cup) nuts, finely chopped
180 ml (¾ cup) single (light) cream
100 g (1 cup) dessicated coconut

1. If the carob balls are for children, skip this part. Marinate raisins in real rum (I use Captain Morgan rum). (You can keep extra raisins marinated in rum in a jar for next time.)
2. Crumble the cake into a bowl.
3. Add the biscuits, rum raisins, nuts, cream and 2 tbs of the coconut. Mix well.
4. Place the rest of the coconut in a deep bowl. Start making balls out of the mixture, 3 cm (1 in) thick or smaller, then roll them in the coconut until fully covered.
5. Cool in refrigerator for 2 hours (optional).

The balls store well in the freezer.

Carob cookies

Makes 35 cookies

Preheat oven to 180° C (350° F).

200 g (7 oz) butter
200 g (1 cup) brown sugar
300 g (2 cups) wholewheat flour, sifted
1 tsp baking powder
1 tbs honey
100 g (¾ cup) carob powder
1 egg

1. Blend the butter and sugar.
2. Add the rest of the ingredients and mix.
3. Roll into small balls and flatten them by pressing with your finger. Place on an oiled tray and bake for 15 minutes.

Almond biscuits

Once you eat these almond biscuits (cookies), you'll never want to eat any other kind!

Makes 40 biscuits (cookies)

Preheat oven to 170° C (340° F).

200 g (7 oz) butter
100 g (½ cup) brown sugar
85 g (1 cup) almonds, finely ground
300 g (2 cups) wholewheat flour
1 egg, beaten
1 tsp vanilla essence (extract)
a pinch of salt
icing sugar (powdered sugar)

1. Mix all the ingredients except the icing sugar, and place in the refrigerator for 1 hour.
2. Separate the dough into two. Roll each part into a long sausage 3–4 cm (1–1 ½ in) thick, then cut into 1 cm (½ in) pieces. Roll each piece into a ball and squeeze so the bottom is flat and the top is round.
3. Oil tray and place the balls on it. Bake for 15 minutes.
4. After the biscuits are cool, sprinkle icing sugar on top.

Hazelnut and lemon slice

Makes 30 slices

You will need a cake tin approximately 23 x 35 cm (9 x 14 in).
Preheat oven to 160° C (320° F).

The base

190 g (1 ¼) cups wholewheat flour
100 g (3 ½ oz) soft butter
1 tsp brown sugar
1 egg, beaten

Blend the flour, butter and sugar. Add the egg and mix in. Oil the cake tin and flatten the dough into it. Bake for 15 minutes.

The topping

3 eggs, beaten
250 g (1 ¼ cups) brown sugar
60 g (¾ cup) coconut
3 tbs wholewheat flour
½ tsp baking powder
½ tsp salt
½ tsp vanilla essence (extract)
170 g (1 cup) hazelnuts, toasted and finely chopped

Mix the ingredients and spread the mixture on the baked dough. Bake for 25 minutes. Take it out of the oven and let it cool.

The glaze

130 g (1 cup) icing sugar (powdered sugar)
juice of half a lemon

Mix the sugar with the lemon and pour on the slice after it has cooled.
Cut it into squares of the desired size.

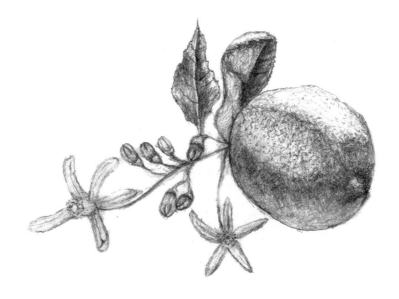

Ginger biscuits

Makes 35-40 biscuits

Preheat oven to 180° C (350° F).

200 g (7 oz) butter
200 g (1 cup) brown sugar
300 g (2 cups) wholewheat flour
1 tsp baking powder
1 tbs honey
120 g (½ cup) crystalised ginger, finely chopped
1 egg, beaten
½ tsp cinnamon, ground
¼ tsp cloves, ground
¼ tsp nutmeg, ground

1. Blend the butter and sugar.
2. Add the rest of the ingredients and mix.
3. Form balls and press them with your finger into biscuit or cookie shape.
4. Place on oiled tray and bake for 15 minutes.

Coconut and oatmeal cookies

These are amazingly delicious. I learned to make them at Nutley Hall, where I worked in the kitchen. At break time I would sneak into the bakery and pinch a few of these freshly baked delights. I felt very satisfied, but naughty.

Makes 35 biscuits (cookies)

Preheat oven to 150° C (300° F).

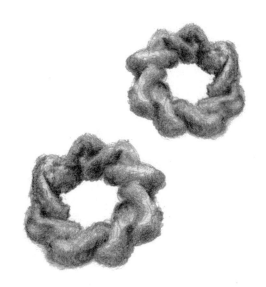

2 tbs lemon juice
1 tsp bicarbonate (baking) soda
1 tbs honey
300 g (2 cups) wholewheat flour
150 g (¾ cup) brown sugar
120 g (1 ½ cups) dessicated coconut
100 g (1 ¼ cups) oatmeal
250 g (9 oz) soft butter
½ tsp cinnamon
a pinch of salt

1. Mix the bicarbonate (baking) soda and lemon juice in a cup. Add the honey and stir.
2. Mix all the other ingredients in a medium-sized bowl. Add the soda mixture and combine by hand until the dough is even.
3. Form little balls in your hand, 3–4 cm (1–1 ½ in) wide. Then press them so they are 1 cm (½ in) thick.
4. Place on an oiled tray 2 cm (½ in) apart (they will spread in the oven).
5. Bake for 20–25 minutes, until the biscuits (cookies) turn golden.
6. Take out of the oven and cool for 2 minutes, then lift them from the tray while still hot. Store when fully cooled.

Tahini biscuits

Makes 20–25 biscuits

Preheat oven to 180° C (350° F).

100 g (3 ½ oz) butter
100 g (½ cup) brown sugar
100 g (½ cup) tahini
½ tsp vanilla essence (extract)
150 g (1 cup) wholewheat flour
½ tsp baking powder

1. Whip the butter and sugar.
2. Add the tahini, vanilla, flour and baking powder. Mix.
3. Form little balls and press them on top.
4. Place them on baking paper on a greased baking tray (sheet) and cook for 15 minutes.
5. Cool them.
6. Take gently off the tray.

Oat, raisin and walnut cookies

Makes 60 small cookies

Preheat oven to 150° C (300° F).

240 g (3 cups) oatmeal
150 g (1 cup) wholewheat flour
150 g (5 oz) butter
300 g (1 ½ cups) brown sugar
60 ml (¼ cup) water
150 g (1 cup) raisins
1 tsp vanilla essence (extract)
120 g (1 cup) walnuts, chopped
1 egg, beaten
80 g (½ cup) sesame seeds
40 g (½ cup) dessicated coconut

1. Mix all the ingredients.
2. Form small balls and press them flat with your finger.
3. Place on an oiled tray and bake for 15 minutes, until the cookies turn golden.

Blintzes (Hungarian pancakes)

Makes 12–14 pancakes

150 g (1 cup) wholewheat flour
2 eggs, beaten
500 ml (2 cups) water or milk
4 tbs sunflower oil
a pinch of salt
extra oil for frying

1. Place the flour, eggs and a bit of the water or milk in a bowl. Mix with a whisk. Add the rest of the ingredients and keep whisking until you get a smooth mixture.
2. Cool in refrigerator for an hour.
3. Heat some oil in a frying pan or skillet and pour half a ladleful of the mixture into the pan. Fry. Flip and fry other side.

Sweet toppings for blintzes or pancakes

Makes 10 portions

Honey and butter sauce

100 g (3 ½ oz) butter
2–3 tbs honey

Melt the butter on low heat, then add the honey and mix well.

Home-made halva spread

3 tbs tahini
1 tbs honey

Mix the tahini and honey.

This spread makes great sweet sandwiches.

Omama's chocolate sauce

See page 123.

For a nutty chocolate taste, add 120 g (1 cup) of well-chopped
walnuts or hazelnuts (or if you have a food processor,
put the sauce and nuts in it and blend).

Rich granola (v)

Granola is a very nourishing, and much cheaper, alternative to industrial cereals.

Makes 12 cups of granola

Preheat the oven to 150° C (300° F).

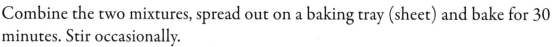

400 g (5 cups) oatmeal
160 g (1 cup) sesame seeds
60 g (½ cup) almonds, whole   } Mix.
120 g (1 cup) walnuts or pecans, whole
75 g (1 cup) dessicated coconut
160 g (1 cup) flax seeds

240 ml (1 cup) honey
125 ml (½ cup) sunflower oil   } Mix.
60 ml (¼ cup) water
1 tbs cinnamon

Combine the two mixtures, spread out on a baking tray (sheet) and bake for 30 minutes. Stir occasionally.

Serve with yogurt, milk, soy (or almond, or oat) milk, orange juice, or by itself as an all-day snack.

You can also add dried fruits to the cooled granola.

From the sun's bright shining,
From the love of the stars,
From the heart of the Earth,
From the flow of the rain,
From the breathing of the air,
God weaves and creates
Food and drink
For mankind to share.

Menus for Children

Nourishing our children

Children's nutrition is an issue that deeply occupies parents today, and with good reason.

It seems that from a young age children prefer food that is completely different from the food that their parents put on the table. Children love simple food with one colour, taste and texture – 'clean' food, such as plain rice, soup without vegetables, and pasta without sauce. Maybe this is their reaction to the abundance of stimulation surrounding them. The world today is full of different products in every type, colour, texture and shape, and not necessarily of good quality. When this abundance touches the most intimate, internal place – food – children choose monk-like simplicity.

Parents are often filled with feelings of anger and frustration when faced with picky children who time and again ask for the same regular, boring dishes. They don't understand the source of the problem. The truth is that the child's soul is still directly connected to the cosmic forces. Mother Earth is one of them, and food comes from her. The Earth now suffers a severe imbalance, and this influences the production of nourishing foodstuff. The earth is tired and worn out from the chemicals and poisons that flow over her. One half of the world throws away food and has an unnecessary abundance of varieties of food, while the other half of the world suffers terrible hunger – and this is just the tip of the iceberg. Maybe children's relationship with food reflects this imbalance?

Another problem that anxious parents struggle with is that even among the abundance it is hard to find food that has a highly nutritious quality and is filled with life forces. Many food products are processed and ready for fast use. Although these products save preparation time and may appear to fulfil our nutritional needs – as specified on the packet – there is no doubt that they are far removed from the simplicity and freshness of good organic food.

My unequivocal recommendation is to create a house that is free from 'bad' food: processed food, food filled with preservatives, prepared food or partially prepared food that has no trace of life forces, and sweets. It is not possible as parents to consume 'bad' food and at the same time to expect your child to eat nutritious food. The child reflects your connection to the world in a deep way. If you are clear in a particular aspect, then your children will also be clear. Every place where you have fears or doubts, or where you yourselves are addicted to 'bad' food, you will find yourselves at war with your children. You need to be able to stand for the food that you bring into your house.

If there is a variety of healthy food on the table, children will be exposed to an assortment of tastes and may learn to also eat your vegetable pie. There is nothing like the sight of other people eating to inspire courage and willingness to try new flavours. My neighbour told me that her daughter flatly refused to try her orange soup. Then one day she ate dinner at the neighbour's house, tasted orange soup, and returned home to report that in fact she loves it.

Creativity and abundant patience will help you to create a healthy atmosphere around your dinner table. Remember that children are nourished from the atmosphere as well as from the food – happiness, lightness, colourfulness and creativity are no less nourishing than wholewheat flour and organic carrots.

Through food we allow the world to enter our being – the air, the earth, the water and the warmth of the sun, as well as all of the active forces and materials in the world. Eating is a way to form a connection with the world. Problems with food arise when we as parents are filled with fears and anxieties about the outside world. Be careful not to pass on to your children a sense that the outside world is hostile, dangerous and bad, even if we are only talking about food. If the neighbours or your children's grandparents serve food that is not healthy or nutritious, it presents a dilemma for you. You can talk to these neighbours or grandparents and ask them to respect your worldview, but do not under any circumstances make an issue out of it in front of your child. The confusion will cause greater damage than sweets or an unhealthy snack. Children need to understand that their neighbours and grandparents also love them, even if these neighbours and grandparents behave and think differently from their parents in relation to food.

Try not to create the feeling that you are keeping bad, dangerous food away from your house and from your children; instead cultivate the idea that you prefer nutritious, healthy food. If you take your children to shop in small, intimate whole-food stores from a young age, they will understand your message: that you support the building of a healthier world, where you are happy to pay people who grow and produce good food for you. Focusing on the positive will give your child the feeling that the world is ultimately a good, friendly place that is filled with miracles and wonders. The taste of sweets is one of them and in the right measure it does not harm anyone.

Small children love to imitate the actions of adults in their environment. The kitchen is an especially fascinating place: it is filled with interestingly sized pots and pans and with many different materials, textures, colours and smells. There are appealing things to do in the kitchen: mixing, stirring, chopping, squeezing, dicing, and even washing the dishes. Your children will want, and will love, to help whoever is cooking. Give your children a small apron to wear and buy them a small footstool so they can reach the counters. Allow them to help with every activity – even if it then takes a bit longer. Create a quiet atmosphere in the kitchen – without radio or television – and bring focused energy to what you're doing. Be present! Observe the colour, the shape, the smell and the texture of the ingredients that you are using and be amazed by them. In this way you will give your children the simple message that the world is beautiful and diverse.

Nothing can equal food that is created together in a happy, loving, intimate environment. Your children will remember these moments in the kitchen for the rest of their lives: the chaos, and the smell of the cake that needs to be taken out of the oven, as well as the skills that they learn through imitation and play.

A colourful meal for children

ORANGE (PUMPKIN) SOUP (SEE PAGE 115)

CORN BURGERS

ROAST POTATOES AND SWEET POTATOES (V)

QUICK AND SIMPLE VEGETABLE STEW (V)

CHOCOLATE INDULGENCE

Corn burgers

450 g (16 oz) sweetcorn, fresh or frozen
4–5 tbs wholewheat flour
3 eggs, beaten
2 medium onions, finely chopped
half a bunch dill, finely chopped (optional)
salt and pepper
sunflower oil for frying

Mix all the ingredients together, except the oil. Divide the mix into 30 burgers. Flatten slightly. Heat the oil and fry each burger on both sides until golden. Drain on a paper towel.

These are good served with sweet and sour sauce (see page 275).

Roast potatoes and sweet potatoes (V)

Serves 4–6

Preheat oven to 180° C (350° F).

2 large potatoes, unpeeled, cut into strips
2 medium sweet potatoes, unpeeled, cut into strips
5 tbs olive oil
fresh rosemary
salt

1. Place the potatoes and sweet potatoes in a baking dish. Pour the olive oil on top, then sprinkle with rosemary leaves.
2. Bake for 45 minutes, until the potatoes become golden.
3. Before serving add salt.

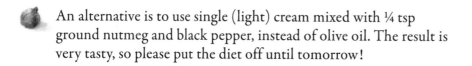

An alternative is to use single (light) cream mixed with ¼ tsp ground nutmeg and black pepper, instead of olive oil. The result is very tasty, so please put the diet off until tomorrow!

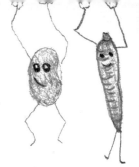

Quick and simple vegetable stew (V)

This dish should have crunchy vegetables. Keep the cooking times short, as suggested!

Serves 4

olive oil for sautéing
1 onion, cut into quarters
} Sauté for 5 minutes.

1 small sweet pepper (bell pepper), cut into strips
1 medium carrot, finely sliced
4 garlic cloves, chopped
} Add and keep frying for 5 minutes

2 tomatoes, cut into little cubes
quarter of a cauliflower or broccoli, separated into little florets
60 ml (¼ cup) water
} Add and cook for a further 10 minutes, stirring occasionally. Turn off heat.

½ cup fresh basil, chopped
} Add at the end.

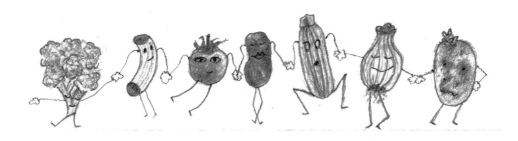

Chocolate indulgence

This dessert uses cornflour (cornstarch), which has no nutritional value, but it is still better than a dessert bought in a shop. I recommend making chocolate indulgence together with children. The experience of cooking it develops their willingness to prepare yummy things at home!

When it's cold outside, you can serve it hot as a thick chocolate drink.

Serves 6–8

4 cups milk
2 tbs cocoa powder
4 tbs brown sugar
3 tbs cornflour (cornstarch)
¼ cup water

Optional additions

zest of an orange, grated
1 tsp vanilla essence (extract)
whipped cream

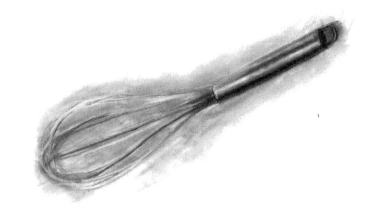

1. Mix the cornflour with the cold water until it is totally smooth. Set aside.
2. Boil the milk. Turn off the heat.
3. Mix the cocoa with the sugar. Add some hot milk to it, mix well and pour it all into the pan of hot milk. Turn on the heat. (You've actually made hot chocolate.)
4. Add the cornflour mixture to the 'hot chocolate'. Using a whisk to prevent lumps, stir constantly until the mixture thickens and becomes mousse-like. Turn off the heat.
5. Add the orange zest or vanilla essence, or both for a heavenly effect. Mix well.
6. Cool the chocolate mix, while whisking from time to time to stop a thick skin forming on the top.
7. Whip the cream. Serve the dessert in a nice glass with the cream on top.

The Pink Kindergarten's meal

HUNGARIAN GOULASH (V)

BROWN RICE (SEE PAGE 68)

HUNGARIAN CUCUMBER SALAD (SEE PAGE 31)

APPLE OR PLUM CRUMBLE

Hungarian goulash (V)

In the first anthroposophical kindergarten established in Jerusalem (The Pink Kindergarten), which my son was lucky enough to attend for two years, the parents take turns to cook. I cooked Hungarian goulash. I replaced the beef or chicken with tofu (with a thousand apologies to my grandmother, who would surely turn in her grave at the thought of my tofu goulash).

The children loved this dish, which was accompanied by the appropriate grain of the day. The parents received positive reports about the goulash from their children. As a result, a few busy parents asked whether I could cook instead of them. Being a quite poor state-school teacher at that time, I happily agreed to some extra money. So, three times a month the kindergarten children ate Hungarian tofu goulash. We were all happy and well nourished!

Serves 8–10

olive oil for sautéing
2 large onions, chopped

Sauté until golden brown.

4 cloves garlic, crushed
1 large potato, peeled and cubed
1 red pepper (bell pepper), cut into small slices
1 large carrot, diced
1 celery stalk with leaves, finely chopped
300 g (10 oz) tofu, cut into small cubes
1 tsp sweet paprika
½ tsp hot paprika (optional)
480 ml (2 cups) vegetable stock or water

Add to the onion and cook for 20–30 minutes, covered, on low heat, until the potato is soft.

salt to taste
240 ml (½ cup) tomato paste

Add and cook 2–5 minutes.

1 bunch parsley, finely chopped

Add after you turn off the heat.

The goulash is the best the next day, when all the tastes have blended together.

Apple and plum crumble

This is the best crumble I have ever had. It comes from England, and was passed to me by my dear friend Sharon Ivry.

Serves 8–10

You will need a round, 28 cm (11 in) diameter pie dish, or a square one, 24 x 32 cm (9.5 x 11.5 in).

Preheat oven to 150° C (300° F).

The fruit mixture

1 kg (2 lb) apples and plums (about 7–8 pieces of fruit), washed and cut into cubes

120 ml (½ cup) apple juice or freshly squeezed orange juice
1 tbs cinnamon
35 g (¼ cup) raisins
zest of half a lemon, finely grated
juice of a lemon

Put the fruit straight into the baking pan. No need for oiling! Add the other ingredients to the fruits and mix.

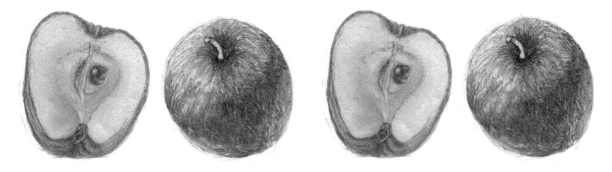

The crumble

    200 g (7 oz) melted butter
    80 g (1 cup) oatmeal or rolled oats
    200 g (1 cup) brown sugar
    150 g (1 cup) wholewheat flour
    115 g (1 cup) finely ground walnuts, or almonds, or pecans

Mix in a bowl and crumble it over the top of the fruit.

    Bake the crumble 30–40 minutes until the top is slightly brown. Some people like it very baked.

    Serve hot with ice cream (ginger flavour is great!) (see page 93), or with vanilla sauce (see page 255), or with cream.

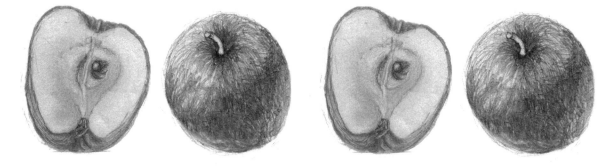

Moving

During my childhood we moved houses twice a year. In the late spring after the fruit trees stopped showing off their blossoms and diligently turned their strength to the creation of their baby fruit, we moved to the summer house. It was on the top of a hill at the edge of our town, surrounded by vineyards and orchards. In the late autumn, after the grape harvest, when the air was filled with the smell of fermenting grape juice waiting in huge wooden barrels in our basement to turn into wine, we moved back to our winter house. It was in the centre of our town, close to the river.

We called our summer house 'the Hegy', which means 'the mountain'. As soon as the fierce April rains stopped and the dirt road dried enough for a truck to pass, we packed up the house in town. There were no cardboard boxes in those days in Romania, so sheets and blankets were spread on the floor. Into them we piled our clothes, bedding, towels, shoes, books and other most necessary belongings, then a huge knot was formed from the four corners of the sheet. The bigger bowls, pots and pans hosted the smaller ones. Grains, beans and smoked *kolbász* (sausage) that we had not finished in the winter were packed into containers. The fridge was emptied and washed in preparation for the journey. The old gas stove knew that it would not be left behind either.

The packing went on for two days so we all had to live in a peculiar, temporary situation amidst upheaval, finding our way through the items piled up all over the house. The only normal place left was the toilet, to which I loved to escape. We shared it with our Romanian neighbours who lived at the end of the corridor and were thieves, according to mother.

The house was buzzing with nervous adults, who were agitated by us kids running around excited by the whole event. I was the happiest in those two days, knowing that a whole summer lay ahead of me in my beloved garden.

An enormous truck came, always with the same driver, who would not have done this difficult job if he did not know us. First the big kitchen machines went onto the truck, then the furniture, followed by all the piles of filled sheets and blankets that were tucked under and above everything else, wherever possible. The open truck got so full that some of us had to sit on top of all the piles, holding onto them so that they would not fall off.

I loved sitting there, watching the streets of town being devoured one after the other by our slowly moving truck. Finally it crossed the railroad that signalled the end of town and entered the bumpy narrow dirt road that led to my beloved Hegy.

The journey included some heart-quickening moments in which the truck got stuck in a hole in the road, or tilted so much to one side because of the uneven ground that some of our things started falling off. I had to knock hard on the window of the cabin to call the driver to stop. But in the end we arrived.

The old stone house covered with vines was waiting majestically. Before helping to carry all our things in, I ran to my quince tree in the middle of the garden and told her that her winter loneliness was now over because I had arrived. She had been my *zula* (sanctuary) for a few years, ever since I discovered that her branches were wide and strong enough to become the home of a little stool with a pillow on it. After having finished my morning chores, there I would sit most of the day and read Tolstoy, Turgenev, Balzac, Dickens, the Bronte sisters, Cooper's native American stories and an endless amount of pulp fiction. My grandmother's magazine collection from the 1920s *Magyar Lanyok* (Hungarian Women) introduced me to the culture of the post-WW1 years, and filled me with a romanticism impossible to erase even in the hardships of the twenty-first century.

When evening came, all activities exhausted themselves and we all went to bed. I slept in the living room with Omama, my bed under the window. As silence descended on the house, I lay there and looked out to the stars. They seemed mysterious. Lonely shining spots in the dark sky. I did not know then how dark the sky can become and how hard it would be to find the shining stars later in life. But on that first night of the summer holiday, I was the happiest girl in the world.

Busy Cooks

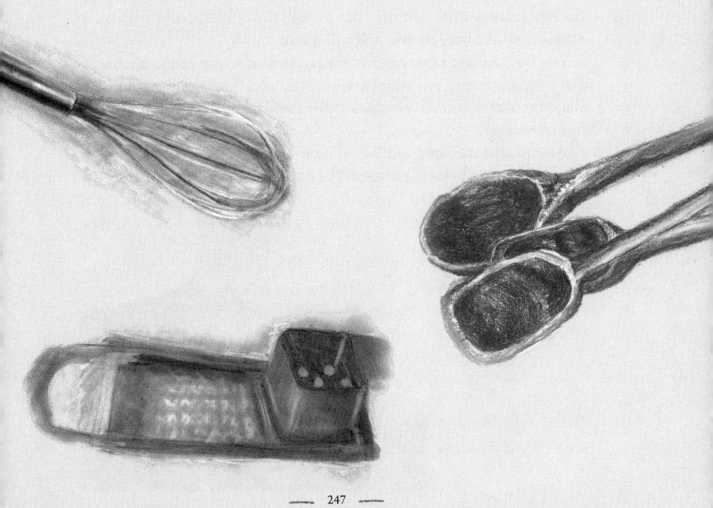

What about mothers?

Until two or three generations ago, cooking was the exclusive responsibility of the mother, along with looking after the children and doing other household tasks. It was taken for granted that there would be food cooked from simple, local ingredients.

Cooking and eating had a specific time and order that was integrated into and inseparable from the pattern of daily life.

Today, with women's liberation and women working outside of the home, the daily activity of cooking is disappearing from our lives. Pre-prepared food, eating out and heating up processed food is becoming more and more common.

These solutions have arisen to answer the needs of the mother who finishes a day at work and then has to start the domestic work, which is experienced as a burdensome and tiring task.

I do not intend to suggest that women should return to the kitchen!!! But I would remind everyone of the blessed and nourishing influence of simple cooking – on all members of the family, but mostly on the cook, him or herself.

And indeed, cooking can be a simple matter, easy to carry out and pleasurable, even before or after work hours.

A tasty and easy meal

OAT GROATS DELIGHT WITH FRIED ONIONS, NUTS AND RAISINS (V)

PASTRY-FREE COURGETTE (ZUCCHINI) QUICHE

LETTUCE AND FENNEL SALAD (V)

BEETROOT (BEET) AND GARLIC SALAD (V)

BAKED PLUM AND CINNAMON DESSERT (V)

VANILLA SAUCE

Oat groats delight with fried onions, nuts and raisins (V)

Serves 4–6

200 g (1 cup) oat groats
420 ml (1 ¾) cups water
salt to taste

} Put in a pot, bring to the boil, lower the heat, cover the pot and cook for 45 minutes.

(You could also do this step earlier in the day, or the night before.)
Meanwhile prepare the onions, nuts and raisins.

olive oil for frying
2 medium onions, chopped

1 tbs brown sugar
2 tbs soy sauce
75 g (½ cup) raisins
60 g (½ cup) nuts, chopped and toasted

} Fry onions until golden. Turn off heat. Add the other ingredients to the onions.

basil or parsley, chopped

When the oat groats are ready, mix them into the onion stew. For decoration, sprinkle oat groats delight with fresh chopped basil or parsley.

Pastry-free courgette (zucchini) quiche

It is amazing that such a simple quiche can be so delicious!

Serves 12–14

You will need a 28 cm (11 in) diameter pie dish.
Preheat oven to 150° C (300° F).

5 large courgettes (zucchinis) (1.3 kg or 3 lb), coarsely grated

olive oil for frying
1 large leek (700 g), sliced, or 3 large onions, chopped

salt
1 bunch of dill or parsley, finely chopped
150 g (1 cup) wholewheat flour
4 eggs, beaten
pinch of black pepper

a handful of sesame and sunflower seeds

1. Mix the courgette (zucchini) with salt. Let it stand for 5 minutes then squeeze out the liquid.
2. Fry the leek or onion in plenty of olive oil until golden.
3. Add the fried leek or onion, dill or parsley, another tsp salt (or to taste), flour, eggs and black pepper to the courgette (zucchini) and mix.
4. Grease the pie dish and pour the mixture into it. Sprinkle the seeds on top.
5. Bake for 40 minutes.

If you'd like a dough base, you can use the pastry from Cheese and vegetable pie, page 181.

For a colourful quiche, place round tomato slices on the top before baking.

Lettuce and fennel salad (V)

Serves 10–12

1 large lettuce, torn into big pieces
1 large carrot, coarsely grated
2 medium radishes, sliced
1 small fennel, finely sliced
¼ small cabbage, finely chopped
50 g (½ cup) bean sprouts
60 ml (⅓ cup) olive oil
5 tbs balsamic vinegar

Place all the vegetables in a bowl and pour the olive oil and vinegar over them. Mix well.

40 g (¼ cup) sunflower seeds, toasted in
soy sauce (see page 85)
80 g (½ cup) black olives

Sprinkle sunflower seeds and olives on top.

Instead of olive oil and balsamic vinegar,
you can use House dressing (see page 58).

Beetroot (beet) and garlic salad (v)

Serves 6

2 large beetroots (beets)
3 tbs olive oil
2 tbs vinegar
1 tsp honey
½ tsp salt
2 spring onions (scallions), chopped
3 cloves garlic, finely chopped
parsley, chopped

1. Put the beetroots (beets) in a pot and cover them with water. Cook until a knife will go through easily. Let them cool a little.
2. Peel them with your hands, rubbing the skin gently with your fingers.
3. Grate them into a bowl.
4. Add the other ingredients except for the parsley, and stir.
5. Decorate the salad with the chopped parsley.

Baked plum and cinnamon dessert (v)

Serves 4–6

500 g (1 lb) black plums or apples (or both) seeded and cut into cubes
75 g (½ cup) raisins or sultanas (golden raisins)
zest of an orange, grated
4 tbs water
¼ tsp cinnamon, ground (optional)
1–2 cloves (optional)

1. Place the fruit, raisins or sultanas (golden raisins) and orange zest in a pot, add 4 tbs water. Cover the pot and cook on low heat until the fruit is soft.
2. Add the cinnamon and 1 or 2 cloves. (Careful! They are very dominant!)
3. Serve warm or cool depending on taste and the season.

Instead of plums and apples it is possible to use other fruits: blueberries, pears, peaches or apricots.

For an absolutely delicious dessert, you can serve it with vanilla cream (see below).

Vanilla sauce

480 ml (2 cups) milk
2 egg yolks
4 tbs brown sugar
zest of a quarter lemon, finely grated
zest of a quarter orange, finely grated
1 tsp vanilla essence (extract) (good quality)
2 tbs wholewheat flour

1. Boil the milk in a pan large enough to hold the rest of the ingredients. Turn off the heat.
2. In a bowl, whip the yolks and sugar until they are nicely blended and fluffy.
3. Add the lemon and orange zest, vanilla essence, and flour. Mix.
4. Using a ladle, add some of the boiled milk to the yolk mixture and stir. I warmly suggest you use a wire whisk, so there will be no lumps. Repeat this until you have finished all the milk. Don't panic, the mixture is meant to become more liquid.
5. Pour the mixture back into the milk pan. Cook, stirring constantly with the whisk, until the mixture thickens.

To make a thinner sauce, use more milk.

To make a **vanilla cream**, add in another yolk and 2 tbs sugar.
After taking off the heat, add 100 g (3 ½ oz) butter.

Fulfilling Dreams

Karma, stuffed cabbage and Harduf's restaurant

Harduf's restaurant was given to me by the cosmos. Before then, I was living in Forest Row, East Sussex, England, studying Waldorf education with an amazing teacher, Brian Masters, and cooking at Nutley Hall. I was part of a cook's study group from Emerson College and had the best life I could have imagined. I had no desire to return to Israel. I could not imagine leaving my housemate, Helen, and her son, William, the cool weather, the rich anthroposophical study, the countryside I had fallen in love with, and all my friends, who had become my family.

But then karma disturbed my perfect life. I had started to lecture on cooking from a spiritual point of view, and my friend Suzanne Hillen suggested I open a healthy café in the village as many people there wanted a place serving good food. I found an investor and we started to hunt for a location. After six months of unsuccessful searching, he said he thought my karma was somewhere else and was blocking our café plans. I was very angry with him, not recognising at all what I know today: when something you really want doesn't happen, that means it should not happen. It was not in my karma. No matter what I did, karma was stronger. Without an investor, there was no café.

A month later I got a letter from the British Home Office announcing that I had to leave the UK by the summer. My whole world collapsed. I so much wanted to stay! But none of my trials succeeded.

When it became clear that we would have to leave, I started to wonder about where to go. A Waldorf school for my then twelve-year-old son, Adam, was an absolute necessity. My mother wanted us to come and live in Budapest, only three hours away from her in Várad. My sister from Toronto offered us an apartment in her home. Both places had Waldorf schools. Still, I couldn't imagine living in the metropolitan Budapest or in yet another new country, Canada, at the age of 42. So I called, as a last option, a great friend in Harduf, Israel, and asked whether there might be a place for Adam in the very crowded and popular Waldorf school there. He told me that a family with a son Adam's age was leaving, and he would make sure Adam was given priority in the waiting list. 'Besides,' he said, 'there is a restaurant in Harduf that is screaming for a mother!'

And so, against our will, we came to Harduf and stayed. Nearly twenty years have passed. The restaurant slowly, slowly turned into my dream café, though very different from the ideas I had of it in Forest Row. The food, the look, the team – who became my family – are perfect. The restaurant is a being with its own will and I sit sometimes after we close and ask it what I should do to make it happier. Every day when I close the door, I thank it for being there in my life. I'm still in love with it! This 'heavenly meal' was born from its request.

Heavenly meal

MUSHROOM AND SPINACH SOUP (V)

STUFFED CABBAGE WITH BEETROOT (BEET),
CARROT AND APPLE SAUCE

FRESH AND CREAMY CUCUMBER SALAD

APPLE CAKE PIE

Mushroom and spinach soup (V)

This is a light, special and yummy soup! It is composed of vegetables that flavour it and a roux, which thickens it.

Serves 10–12

olive oil or butter for sautéing
2 medium onions, finely chopped
400 g (14 oz) fresh spinach, washed well and finely chopped
400 g (14 oz) fresh mushrooms (any kind), washed and sliced
2 litres (4 U.S. pints) stock or water
4 tbs soy sauce

a large handful of dill, finely chopped, for decoration
juice of a lemon

1. In a pot, sauté the onions in the fat until golden.
2. Add the mushrooms and sauté one more minute.
3. Add the spinach and sauté until it softens. Stir from time to time.
4. Add the stock or water, bring to the boil, lower the heat and cook for five minutes.
5. Add the soy sauce.

The roux

4 tbs olive oil
35 g (¼ cup) flour
sweet paprika to taste
salt and black pepper to taste

1. Gently heat the oil, add the flour and fry on low heat, stirring constantly with a wooden spoon, for two minutes. Add the paprika, salt and pepper and stir for one minute.
2. Take out about one cupful of liquid from the soup, add to the roux and mix with a whisk until it becomes a smooth paste. Add a little more soup until the roux mixture becomes liquid enough to be poured into the soup. Once it unites with the soup, it all needs another 5–10 minutes of cooking to thicken.
3. Add lemon juice when serving the soup. Sprinkle chopped dill on top.

A present from God

One day I wanted to introduce a new dish to the restaurant. But I couldn't think of anything. No new dish appeared in my barren brain. I had already begun to despair when one day, after I had closed the restaurant, I sat down at one of the tables, looked around and felt how 'hungry' she was for a new dish. I did not have anything to give her. I rose to leave the table, disappointed, when it arrived: cabbage stuffed with our mixed grains, steamed vegetables and olive oil, accompanied by the most heavenly and unique sauce: freshly squeezed carrot and beetroot (beet) juice with olive oil and vinegar. Before my eyes I saw the beauty of the dish and I tasted its flavour in my mouth.

The mauve colour of the sauce poured over the translucent green cabbage, with a dash of white sour cream on the top and garnished with dill, was an inviting idea for the eye and mouth!

I was very excited and I knew that I was not the one who had invented such a beautiful and perfect dish, but that it was sent as a gift from God. I am happy to pass the gift on to you.

Preparing the stuffed cabbage is labour intensive, so I recommend that you make the full quantity and invite guests, who should come with an appetite. It also keeps well for 5–6 days in the refrigerator.

Stuffed cabbage with beetroot (beet), carrot and apple sauce

Makes 21 portions

First, cook the mixed grains (see page 71), which you will need for the filling. Ideally, do this the day before. You'll need about 750 g (1 ½ lb) cooked weight.

This recipe has three parts:

the cabbage leaves
the filling (mixed grains and sautéd vegetables)
the sauce

Preparing the cabbage

1 or 2 large white or red cabbages, sufficient for 21 roll-able leaves

1. Boil water in a large pot.
2. Cut out the 'heart' of the cabbage (with apologies in our hearts!), which is the white fleshy bit at its base. You can grate it into your salad or add it to your soup or stock.
3. Cook the cabbage for 10–15 minutes, until the outer leaves can easily be removed.
4. Remove the leaves that are soft enough to be rolled without breaking. If you see that they are still too hard, you can throw them back into the boiling water and keep cooking until they are soft, but not mushy. Remember throughout that you have to fill them and roll them.

Continues

The filling

While you are waiting for the cabbage's water to boil, you can prepare the filling!

olive oil for sautéing
1 large leek, washed and finely chopped, or 3 medium onions, finely chopped
4–5 cloves garlic, crushed
5 celery stalks with leaves, finely sliced
4 medium carrots, roughly grated
1 tbs caraway seeds
1 bunch dill, finely chopped
salt and pepper

1. In a large pot, sauté the leek or onions in the olive oil until golden.
2. Add the garlic, celery and carrots and sauté for another 5–10 minutes. Turn off the heat.
3. Add caraway seeds, dill, salt and pepper.

60 g (½ cup) pine kernels, toasted in the oven, or 60 g (½ cup) walnuts, chopped and toasted, or 200 g (7 oz) tofu, grated
750 g (1 ½ lb) cooked mixed grains
3 eggs, beaten

1. Add the nuts or tofu and the mixed grains to the sautéd onion and vegetables. Mix. Taste and add more salt if it needs. (At this point, you will find yourself starting to eat the filling because it is so delicious and nourishing! Make sure to leave some to go inside the cabbage leaves! On another day you can make just the grains and vegetables into a meal with a rich salad.)
2. Add the eggs and mix well.

Stuffing the cabbage

1. Place 2–3 tbs filling near the base of each cabbage leaf.
2. Fold in the two sides and roll tightly, starting from the base.
3. Place the stuffed leaves in a pot, tight together, row after row, with the closing of the stuffed leaf lying at the bottom of the pot in order to prevent the leaf unrolling and the filling falling out.

The sauce

500 ml (2 ¼ cups) beetroot (beet) juice
500 ml (2 ¼ cups) carrot juice
120 ml (½ cup) concentrated apple juice
120 ml (½ cup) apple cider vinegar
120 ml (½ cup) olive oil

1. Mix all the sauce ingredients.
2. Pour the sauce gently over the stuffed and rolled leaves.
3. Bring the pot to the boil, lower the heat and simmer gently for 40–50 minutes with the lid on.

Stuffed cabbage is tastiest the next day, after the sauce has had enough time to befriend the filling.

The Hungarians, who make the filling with minced pork, eat it with sour cream on the top. (Apologies to my Jewish ancestors! Jews do not eat pork and do not ever mix meat with dairy. These are two of the important rules for being kosher.)

If you make this frighteningly complicated dish, I would like to know how it comes out. Make sure you write to me!

Fresh and creamy cucumber salad

Serves 8–10

4 medium cucumbers, roughly grated
1 medium red onion, finely chopped
120 ml (½ cup) sour cream or cream cheese
120 ml (½ cup) yogurt
half a bunch parsley, finely chopped
quarter bunch mint leaves, finely chopped
6 garlic cloves, crushed
5 tbs olive oil
salt to taste

a few whole olives
mint leaves to garnish

Mix all the ingredients, except the olives and mint leaves, in a bowl.
Decorate the top of the salad with the olives and mint leaves.

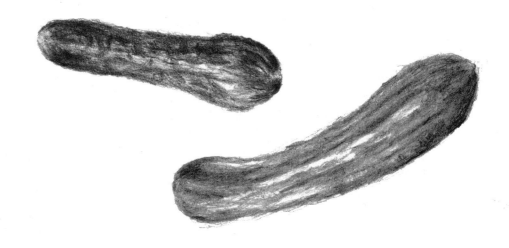

Apple cake pie

Serves 10–12

You will need a 28 cm (11 in) diameter cake tin, greased.
Preheat the oven to 150° C (300° F).

The dough

80 g (1 cup) oatmeal
300 g (2 cups) wholewheat flour
150 g (1 ¼ cups) brown sugar
200 g (7 oz) very soft butter
1 egg, beaten

The filling

1 kg (2 lb) cooking or sour apples, seeded and finely sliced or roughly grated
juice and grated zest of a lemon
1 tsp dry ginger powder
1 tbs cinnamon, or to taste
60 g (½ cup) walnuts or pecans, chopped
75 g (½ cup) raisins

Continues

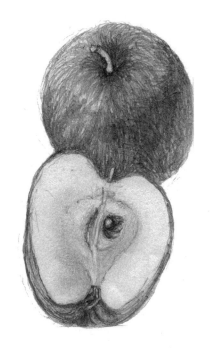

1. In a bowl, with your hands, mix together well all the ingredients of the dough except the egg, working the butter into the dry ingredients with your fingertips. Divide it into two. Press one half of the dough into the bottom of your oiled and lined cake tin with your fingers. If there is a lot of dough, you can press some up the sides of the tin.
2. Mix the filling and put it onto the dough.
3. Add the egg to the other half of the dough, mix well, roll it out with a rolling pin and place it onto the apple filling.
4. Bake for 50 minutes.

You can serve it with home-made ice cream (see page 93), or vanilla sauce (see page 255), or whipped cream.

The cake is delicious with plums or pears as alternatives to apples.

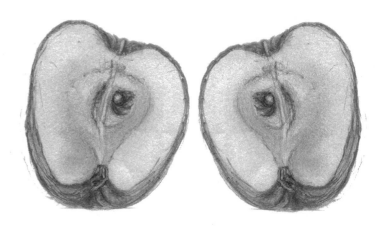

The chosen meal

Sometimes we decide to introduce a new dish to the restaurant. To do this we need to remove one of the existing dishes. One day I decided to part with the almond burgers. The burgers were the only dish that I inherited from the people of Harduf who started the restaurant, and I felt that their time had passed.

Not two days had gone by before customers arrived at the restaurant from Tel Aviv (90 minutes away) and were disappointed to find that there were no almond burgers. I offered them stuffed butternut squash, which they enjoyed, but when they left they wanted to know whether next time they came there would be almond burgers. I assured them that there would be.

I understood then that some dishes will remain forever.

The chosen meal

GREEN SPINACH AND BROCCOLI SOUP (V)

WINTERY STEW (V)

ALMOND BURGERS

SWEET AND SOUR SAUCE (V)

A BASIC SALAD (SEE PAGE 57)

CABBAGE AND SESAME SALAD (V)

ZIV'S CHEESECAKE

HIBISCUS AND APPLE JUICE DRINK (V)

Green spinach and broccoli soup (V)

This soup has a beautiful green colour, rich in leaves and roots.

Serves 16 (makes 4 litres – 8 U.S. pints)

2 medium onions, finely chopped
1 large leek, cleaned and chopped
250 g (9 oz) fresh spinach or Swiss chard, washed and chopped
6 celery stalks with leaves, chopped
500 g (1 lb) broccoli, broken into florets
1 kohlrabi, peeled and cut into cubes
½ tbs caraway seeds
stock or water, an amount that covers the vegetables
400 ml (1 ½ cups) coconut milk or 240 ml (1 cup) single (light) cream (optional)
half a bunch fresh dill, or fresh coriander (cilantro), finely chopped
salt and pepper to taste

1. Put all the cut vegetables and the caraway seeds into a pot. Cover them with water or stock.
2. Cook until all the vegetables are very soft.
3. Blend the soup with a hand blender or food processor. If you don't have these gadgets, the soup is less green but just as delicious.
4. Add the coconut milk or cream if you want it, and the chopped dill or coriander (cilantro), and season to taste.

If you like biting into soup, take some of it out before blending and then add it back to the pot afterwards.

You can serve this soup with home-made croutons (see page 84).

For decoration, serve with a dill sprig on top.

Wintery stew (V)

On a wintery Shabbat or Sunday, you can invite family, friends and neighbours and multiply the quantity of this stew. I recommend you cook it in an iron or clay pot.

Serves 6–8

The vegetables

4 medium onions, cut into four, or 2 leeks, chopped, or half onions, half leek
half a garlic bulb, roughly chopped
1 medium carrot, thickly sliced
2 celery stalks with leaves, chopped
1 celeriac, chopped into large chunks
4 cabbage leaves, cut into thin strips
1 large sweet potato, cut into cubes
quarter of a cauliflower, broken into florets
1 litre (4 cups) water or stock
80 ml (⅓ cup) soy sauce
120 ml (½ cup) olive oil

The grains

100 g (½ cup) brown rice
100 g (½ cup) oat groats
50 g (¼ cup) barley
50 g (¼ cup) millet
40 g (½ cup) quinoa

1. Put all the vegetables except the sweet potato and the cauliflower into a pot. Add the water or stock, soy sauce and olive oil.
2. Mix all the grains and add to the pot.
3. Bring to boil, cover the pot, lower the heat and cook for 30 minutes.
4. Add the sweet potato and cauliflower and cook for 30 more minutes.

You can add a big beetroot (beet) cut into cubes (if it's organic, wash it well but don't peel it). Your stew will be red and really delicious!

If you want the stew to be dominated by vegetables rather than grains, add more vegetables.

Lately, Fatma has been adding 100 g (½ cup) white or butter beans, soaked for one day and cooked until soft. Add them at the beginning.

Almond burgers

Makes 25–30 burgers

If baking, flour a baking tray (sheet) and preheat oven to 150° C (300° F).

300 g (10 ½ oz) almonds, finely ground
half a bunch parsley, finely chopped
1 big carrot, finely grated
1–2 celery stalks with leaves, finely chopped
2 medium onions, finely chopped
10 garlic cloves, crushed
1 tsp salt
1 egg, beaten
75 g (½ cup) wholewheat flour or *matzah* flour
black pepper

flour for rolling
sunflower oil for frying

1. If you have a food processor it will be an easy job: first finely grind the almonds and put them in a big bowl, then finely grate all the vegetables, too, in the food processor. Add them to the almonds. Or, if you do not have a food processor, make sure you grate all the vegetables or chop them very finely.
2. Add all the other ingredients, except the extra flour and the sunflower oil, and mix well.
3. After you have mixed all the ingredients, wet your hands, form burgers (4 cm –1 ½ in – across, 1 cm – ½ in – thick) and place them on a floured tray. Fry them in sunflower oil until both sides are lightly brown, or bake them for 20–25 minutes.

 These burgers are also good without celery, if you prefer.

 Serve with sweet and sour apple sauce (see page 166) or
sweet and sour sauce (see next page).

Sweet and sour sauce (V)

The sauce goes well with almond burgers (see previous page) and in fact with any kind of burger. It keeps for months in the refrigerator and can be used as a perfect alternative to tomato sauce (ketchup). Make it with your children; they will love it!

Makes about 450 g (1 lb)

240 ml (1 cup) water
100 g (½ cup) brown sugar
120 ml (¼ cup) apple cider vinegar
4 tbs tomato paste
3 tbs soy sauce

Bring to a boil, lower the heat and simmer for 2 minutes.

1 flat tsp cornflour (cornstarch)
3 tbs water

Mix until smooth.

Add the cornflour mixture to the simmering sauce, stirring constantly with a hand whisk.

Cook for another 2–3 minutes until the sauce thickens.

Cabbage and sesame salad (V)

Note that you need time for marinating.

Serves 6–8

quarter of a white cabbage, finely sliced
1 celery stalk, without leaves, finely sliced
150 g (1 cup) sweetcorn, cooked
sesame dressing (see page 59)
toasted sesame seeds

Put all the vegetables in a bowl, add the dressing, mix and marinate for a few hours before serving.

How to toast sesame seeds

Stir them constantly with a wooden spoon in a frying pan or skillet on low heat with 1 tsp salt for 10 minutes (no oil). Crush them in a mortar while hot or just sprinkle them on the salad.

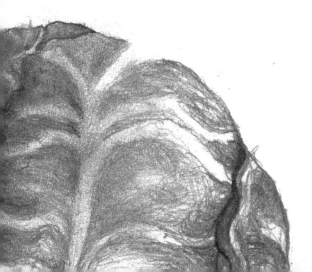

Ziv's cheesecake

This is the best cheesecake that I know. It is a bit 'junky' because of the chocolate and cocoa, but if you only eat it occasionally it is fine in my opinion.

Serves 12–20

You will need a round, 26 cm (10 in) diameter cake tin, greased.
Preheat the oven to 160° C (320° F).

The base

200 g (7 oz) good biscuits (cookies), finely crushed
100 g (3 ½ oz) walnuts, finely ground
2 tbs cocoa or carob powder
2 tbs brown sugar
100 g (3 ½ oz) butter, melted

1. Combine all the ingredients except the butter in a food processor, or by hand in a bowl.
2. Add the melted butter, mix.
3. Flatten the dough by hand into the cake tin.
4. Bake for 10 minutes. Cool.

Continues

The filling

200 g (7 oz) white chocolate
240 ml (1 cup) whipping cream, divided in half to 2 portions
4 eggs
200 g (1 cup) brown sugar
500 g (1 lb) labane (see page 63) or cream cheese

1. Melt the white chocolate in a pan with one half of the cream while whisking. Cool.
2. Whip the eggs and sugar.
3. Add to the egg mixture: the labane or cheese, the other half a cup of cream and the melted chocolate. Mix.
4. Pour the cheese mixture onto the base. Bake 45–60 minutes until the cake feels firm. Take it out of the oven (keep the oven on).

The icing

480 ml (2 cups) sour cream
50 g (¼ cup) sugar
1 tbs vanilla essence (extract)

1. Mix.
2. Pour the icing onto the cheesecake, and spread evenly.
3. Bake for a further 10 minutes. Cool.

Hibiscus and apple juice drink (V)

Makes approximately 2 litres (4 U.S. pints)

1 tbs hibiscus flowers or 3 hibiscus tea bags
3 cloves
3–4 cinnamon sticks
2 litres (4 U.S. pints) water

1 litre (2 U.S. pints) water
450–500 ml (1 U.S. pint) concentrated apple juice (adjust to taste, for sweetness)

1. Put all the ingredients except the apple juice and 1 litre of water into a pot. Bring to the boil. Lower the heat and cook for 15 minutes.
2. Strain out the cloves and cinnamon.
3. Add the remaining 1 litre water and the concentrated apple juice to the boiled liquid. Leave to cool.

In the summer
Add pieces of lemon to the juice.
If you have mint in the garden, add that too.

In the winter
Serve warm and add 1 apple sliced or diced. You can also add slices of orange or lemon. For an even more interesting and delicious taste, add some herbs like melissa, lemon balm or lemon verbena to the boiling water with the hibiscus for the last 5 minutes.

Harduf's restaurant

The team: Fatma, Jutka, Keren

Jutka

Gratitude

Since we have been blessed with a swimming pool in Harduf, the summer has turned into a bearable season. Every day I wake up just in time to say goodbye to the last shades of night and greet the big orange ball rising from the hill opposite my house. The walk to the pool and my early morning swim has become a ritual that I would not miss for anything in the world.

On the way to the pool I pass pomegranate trees rich with red round fruit, looking as if they have just stepped out of the Garden of Eden. The lush herb garden next to them, with thyme, sage, lemongrass, mint, basil and oregano, could pull me into the illusion I am standing in heaven, were I not hearing the loud shrieks of the hens and cocks from the nearby chicken shed. As I come closer to see the reason for all the hurly-burly, I catch sight of a fox cub rounding the shed, hoping for a tasty breakfast. Seeing me, he stops for a moment and looks straight into my eyes, as if asking for help. But realising quickly whose side I am on, he takes his starving look back into the forest. I reach the pool with a feeling of bliss for this morning.

While I do my laps, some of my loved ones from the other world visit me. I realise how my busy life blocks their way so that they must take any opportunity of peace to come and meet me, when I swim or go for a walk or just sit quietly at home. My time with them is like eating, drinking and breathing. It comes from a place in which I let go of the pain of loss and realise that they are still there in a different shape. Each one of them is interested in a different aspect of my life: Mother asks about food and I always feel sorry for her that she cannot eat anymore; Father just assures me of his protective presence; Safta wants to know about my love life; and Caz, my dear cook friend who taught me so much about nutrition, asks about my cooking courses.

On my way home from the pool I see Gonen going to the school. He teaches a small class of children with severe learning difficulties. His parents are also Hungarian and as we say '*jò reggelt*' (good morning), we smile at each other. I wish him a fruitful year with his class and as I go on I wonder if his and my parents ever met on a path in that distant country, and greeted each other with the same '*jò reggelt*' and wished each other a happy new year.

When I pass by the magic garden I pick some pomegranates for juice and a bunch of herbs for tea. A deep gratitude settles in my heart for the people who created this place, for the ones who carry it on and for my destiny, which brought me here.

KIBBUTZ HARDUF RESTAURANT AND JUTKA'S B&B

Contact details:
www.harduf.org.il/rest
Email: rest@harduf.org.il

Top: The family with
mother in her bra
Left Omama
Right: Aunt Teri
Bottom right: Mother
with her roses
Bottom left: The Hegy

Index